The Diary of Lieutenant von Bardeleben and Other von Donop Regiment Documents

Translated by

Bruce E. Burgoyne

HERITAGE BOOKS
2007

HERITAGE BOOKS
AN IMPRINT OF HERITAGE BOOKS, INC.

Books, CDs, and more—Worldwide

For our listing of thousands of titles see our website at
www.HeritageBooks.com

Published 2007 by
HERITAGE BOOKS, INC.
Publishing Division
65 East Main Street
Westminster, Maryland 21157-5026

Copyright © 1998 Bruce E. Burgoyne

All rights reserved. No part of this book may be reproduced or transmitted in any form or by any means, electronic or mechanical, including photocopying, recording or by any information storage and retrieval system without written permission from the author, except for the inclusion of brief quotations in a review.

International Standard Book Number: 978-0-7884-1054-7

Contents

List of Illustrations *v*

Preface *vii*

Introduction *ix*

An Anonymous Hessian Diary: Probably the Diary of Lieutenant Johann von Bardeleben of the Hesse-Cassel von Donop Regiment
    Johann Heinrich von Bardeleben *2*
    Introduction *3*
    An Anonymous Diary *5*

The Church Book of Georg Christoph Coester, Chaplain of the Hesse-Cassel von Donop Regiment
    Georg Christoph Coester *116*
    Introduction *117*
    Born and Baptized of the Illustrious von Donop Regiment During the Time I Served as Chaplain *122*
    List of those Persons whom I Married during the Time I Served as Chaplain *128*
    Register of Children Baptized in 1782 *137*
    Supplement *160*

Journal of the Hesse-Cassel von Donop Regiment, Maintained by Regimental Quartermaster Johann Georg Zinn
    Johann Georg Zinn *162*
    Introduction *163*
    Journal of the Illustrious von Donop Regiment (later) the von Knyphausen Regiment *164*

Index *187*

Illustrations

1. Substitution Code used by Lt. Bardeleben *facing x*

2. Von Donop Regiment Re-enactors *facing 1*

3. A Regimental Chaplain *facing 115*

4. Von Donop Regiment Re-enactors *facing 161*

Preface

In looking over material which I have translated but not yet published in book form, I realized that I had three documents which complimented one another and would also demonstrate how documents of seemingly limited value develop an importance by verifying information in other documents. This supporting significance is demonstrated by the interlocking information in these three documents. I have included them in the following order. First, an anonymous diary written by a young officer of the Hesse-Cassel von Donop Regiment. From the contents of the diary it appears that he probably was seventeen or eighteen years old when he departed from Germany. Furthermore, it appears that he may have been opposed to the then common practice of selling soldiers into foreign service. He even used coded entries to conceal his innermost feelings. Although he did not sign the diary nor indicate his name in any way in the diary, the information which he recorded, allowed me to identify him with certainty, when combined with information from the two other documents included in this volume.

The next document is Chaplain Georg Christoph Coester's Church Book. Church books make the suffering of the common soldier come to life, and the information contained therein gives a much better understanding of those former enemies. In this instance it also provides the information by which the author of the diary can be identified as Lieutenant Johann Heinrich von Bardeleben.

Finally, the third document is the journal of the von Donop Regiment, maintained by the Regimental Quartermaster Johann Georg Zinn. Although not a very detailed journal, it does provide the names of regimental officers, the names of ships on which they traveled, and confirms that both von Bardeleben and Chaplain Coester were members of the von Donop Regiment.

Editorial Procedures

In making these translations I have altered the method of recording dates so as to provide a uniformity. A letter e has been used after the vowels a, o, and u to indicate an umlaut in the diary. Parentheses are as used by the German authors and my comments and identifying information are enclosed in brackets. I have not though it necessary to provide a bibliography.

Acknowledgments

As always, Inge Auerbach and Otto Froehlich's *Hessische Truppen im amerikanischen Unabhaengigkeitskrieg (HETRINA)*, Marburg, 1972-1976, has been my primary source for identification of military personnel from Hesse-Cassel. I am indebted to Georg Jahn and Brigitte Heinicke for some of the information in the section on Chaplain Coester and to Waltari Bergmann, who may have done the research and prepared the foreword to publication of Coester's Church Book. Donald Londahl-Smidt obtained the copy of the anonymous diary from which I made my translation, and he and Bob Cowan have made corrections and suggestions as to how to improve my translation. Personnel at Heritage Books, Inc. have improved my efforts by providing the all too necessary editing. As ever, my wife Marie deserves credit for reading and rereading the manuscript and giving me encouragement to continue my efforts to make the Hessian documents available to those who have neither the time nor inclination to do so. As always, serious students should return to the original documents to verify my translations.

Bruce E. Burgoyne
Dover, DE 19901

Introduction

The von Donop Regiment was one of fifteen infantry regiments sold into English service by Hesse-Cassel in 1776, to assist in trying to put down the revolt in the American colonies. The regiment sailed to America in 1776 as part of the 1st Division and served in America throughout the war. Although involved in the battles of Long Island, Fort Washington, Brandywine, and Springfield, at no time was it involved in heavy fighting nor did it play a key role in any battle.

The regimental staff normally included a colonel or lieutenant colonel, as regimental commander, a major, adjutant, quartermaster, who kept the regimental journal, or as we would call it, the unit history, an auditor, a surgeon, and for each two regiments, a chaplain.

The five companies usually had a captain commanding, three additional officers, and a total strength of about 120 men. Recruit shipments were sent from Germany each year to fill vacancies within the unit due to deaths and desertions.

I have had eleven books published on the role of the Hessians in the American Revolution prior to this time and I hope the readers will understand something of my motivation. As I continue to work on our former "enemies", it becomes ever more clear that the term enemy carries a connotation of hatred, and I do not think the reader feels a hatred of the Hessians. There is rather a feeling, at least in my case, of sympathy for the men whose leaders placed them in a very dreadful service - fighting and killing, suffering and dying, and without having any stake in the battles, except a desire to survive, or possibly keep their "honor". The readers will note in the following diary that the young man was not pleased with the service he had been sent to perform. The church book which follows will show that it was not only the soldiers who suffered and died, but their families as well.

As I write this, 11 November 1997, it strikes me that this is Veterans' Day, or as it was called when I was a schoolboy, Armistice Day. We observed it as a day to honor those who fell, or served, in "the war to end all wars". Maybe we should have been more conscious of what we were doing. An armistice is only a temporary halt to the fighting, as I and my generation were to learn. I served as an active participant in two wars and was still in service during a third major war. Since I retired, the country has been involved in at least three other outbreaks of violence in which soldiers have died.

Just as I, and probably many others, have ceased hating the Hessians and other subsequent "enemies", I hope that someday we will develop the intelligence and ability to understand our fellow man, before the fighting starts, so that wars will no longer be necessary. Maybe my translations, which hopefully make understanding the Hessians easier, will somehow make it easier to understand all soldiers, everywhere.

Bardeleben Diary

Substitution Code used by Lieutenant Bardeleben

A -	⌐•	K -	⌐•⌐	T -	⌐•
B -	⌐••	L -	⌐••⌐	U -	⌐••
C -	⌐•••	M -	⌐•••⌐	V -	⌐•••
D -	⊔•	N -	⊔•⊔	W -	⌐•
E -	⊔••	O -	⊔••⊔	X -	⌐••
F -	⊔•••	P -	⊔•••⊔	Y -	⌐•••
G -	⌊•	Q -	⌊•⌊	Z -	
H -	⌊••	R -	⌊••⌊		
IJ -	⌊•••	S -	⌊•••⌊		

Members of the von Donop Regiment of re-enactors
(photograph by Bruce Burgoyne.)

An Anonymous Hessian Diary
Probably the Diary
of
Lieutenant
Johann Heinrich von Bardeleben

of the
Hesse-Cassel von Donop Regiment

Johann Heinrich von Bardeleben

Information in *HETRINA* indicates that Johann Heinrich von Bardeleben, an ensign, later second and then first lieutenant in the Hesse-Cassel von Donop Regiment, may have been born in 1760 or 1761 in Cologne. Entries in his diary seem to indicate that he may have been born in 1758 or 1759. However, information from a descendant of one of Johann Heinrich's seven brothers is that Johann Heinrich was born in 1752, and that Johann Heinrich and his oldest brother, Christoph Ludwig, both married girls of the von Gilsa family. My source for this information, John F. DeBardeleben, of Gastonia, North Carolina, is a descendant of Arthur Franz Ferdinand von Bardeleben, who also reported that Johann Heinrich may have been in command of Prussian Artillery at the Battle of Waterloo. This same source noted that Johann Heinrich's mother died on 7 September 1776 and his father on 23 January 1777. Their deaths are mentioned in the pages of the diary which follows.

The brother, Arthur Franz Ferdinand, was a lieutenant in Hesse-Cassel service in the von Ditfurth Regiment. He sailed to America in the same convoy as Johann Heinrich, and, as noted in the diary, the two were able to have brief conversations during the ocean crossing when their ships came close together. Arthur Franz Ferdinand, a younger brother, took his release from service in 1781 and settled in South Carolina.

Bardeleben Diary

Introduction

The following translation was made from a Xerox copy of an anonymous "Hessian" diary, written during the American Revolutionary War, and currently owned by the New York State Library at Albany. The document at the library is obviously a copy of the original as page numbers listed on about every fourth Xerox page run in consecutive sequence. As a result marginal notations may have been made initially either by the author or the individual who made the copy. Also, the author uses two codes in making some diary entries; one of which I have not tried to decipher because it is of insufficient frequency to give even a hint as to its content. The other is a simple substitution code with certain symbols standing for certain letters of the alphabet. A copy of this code is attached at the end of this introduction. Some of the first code references seem to be to pages of either this diary or some other specific book, more likely the latter, but again, the references are of insufficient frequency to yield a quick solution.

The author of this diary appears to have been Johann Heinrich von Bardeleben, as he mentions being in Lieutenant Colonel Karl Philipp Heymell's Company, that a baby was named Heinrich after him, and that he had a brother in the Hesse-Cassel service. A Franz Ferdinand von Bardeleben was in the von Ditfurth Regiment.

The author's account contains more details of the daily garrison life than most of the Hessian diaries, and should appeal to all military buffs. Unfortunately the diary only covers the period from 29 January 1776 to 22 June 1777..

I have added a few footnotes to clarify certain events and expressions, but have not tried to provide an in-depth historical analysis. Again, I caution all serious students of history to use my translation as a quick reference, but to return to the primary document to verify my translation. However, for those who just

Bardeleben Diary

enjoy reading these Hessian diaries and their different accounts of the American Revolution, I hope it will provide a little new information and many hours of entertainment.

An Anonymous Diary

[Written by Lieutenant Johann Heinrich von Bardeleben]

The 29th of February 1776

The von Donop Regiment marched, leaving Homberg at ten o'clock in the morning. Most of the city residents gave us the fondest farewell. Everyone at this moment seemed to show more than the usual emotion. The deepest feelings of pain spread over everyone and their melancholy glances followed us. Inconsolable mothers, weeping wives, and whining children in great numbers followed the regiment and made with this sad scene the most heart-rending impressions. Personally, I could not remain indifferent to the situation and less so as I, possibly more than any other, wished to express my distinct views and ideas. However, I decided to hold my unspoken sorrow as much as possible within my heart and tried not to notice the mixture of pleasure and pain that I felt. Anyone who knows how to relieve the sorrow which I felt has my permission to tell me.

We received our night quarters in the villages of Doernhagen, Wollrode, Albhausen, and Coerten. In all these villages the poverty was extensive and they did not merit the least notice.

The 1st of March - To Niederkaufungen and Heiligenrode. These quarters were far more miserable than the others and unfortunately we had to remain in them for a day of rest.

The 3rd of March - We marched into the Electorate of Hannover and to Uschlag and Benterode in the district of Muenden. Here we had adequate quarters. Every farmer was so busy between trying to provide everything for the comfort and feeding of his billeted soldiers that there was no shortage of food and drink, such as beer, brandy, and coffee, but even the greatest surplus. And truly, the kind-hearted people did everything possible for the soldiers. Above all, in their conduct they

Bardeleben's Diary

showed true sympathy for [Code - sold individuals].[1] My quarters were in Benterode with a farmer, whose entire house seemed in a condition of deterioration. At the same time they allowed nothing to interfere, and their cautious and modest situation made me very attentive. Coffee and food were very tasty. I found upon my entering the house that everything was arranged as would be according to the ways of a polished townsman. These good people required nothing more and refused to accept any payment. However, I left something behind for them. The other farmers also took absolutely nothing from the soldiers, but each one had requested. out of kindness, that his guests even take bread and ham for on the march.

The 4th of March - We crossed the Weser at Muenden and marched through the cities of Mengershausen and Volkerode in the district of Muenden. These quarters were no worse than the previous ones. We had hardly arrived here, when the peasants gathered in great crowds to receive their soldiers.[2]

The 5th of March - We crossed the Leine at Goettingen, marched through the cities of Edesheim, Hollenstedt, and Stoeckheim, and again received very good quarters. We remained here for a day of rest on the sixth. Soldiers and peasants considered this to be an exceptionally fortunate day. Everyone got drunk and nothing disturbed them in their pleasure.[3]

The 7th of March - We marched into Brunswick , to Dillegen and Kayser. These quarters were certainly not as good as those in Hannover. At the same time, nothing was
missing of the necessary foodstuffs, and nothing was had without being paid for.

****

1. Coded material in the manuscript has been placed in brackets within the text, with the translation when the code could be deciphered.
2. Obviously a reference meaning the soldiers who were to be billeted in their homes for the night.
3. This is an interesting comment as it seems to indicate a much looser control over the soldiers than would have been expected.

Bardeleben's Diary

Nevertheless, every official or administrator of the villages was given receipts for the provisions which we supposed would be made good to the farmers by the King.

The 8th of March - To Gresdorf, in the district of Calenberg. The entire regiment stayed here. The quarters were especially good. I stayed with a smith of this village, a man who appeared to be of the meanest birth, but with a noble heart. He had cleaned his house and his entire work place as well. He received me in a manner which men of his kind are especially inclined to do and assured me, as he led me into the parlor, that he eagerly awaited the regiment at the edge of town, in order to welcome the officers. Maybe, he continued, you are more hungry than thirsty and would prefer coffee first. His dear wife, of a similar character, then entered the parlor, greeted me, and set the table. The dinner was especially good and consisted of a delicious veal soup, mashed peas with sugar, and sausage, roast veal, butter and cheese, also wine and beer. We sat together at the table and ate with good appetites. This fine reception pleased me all the more as we had a long and difficult march today. Upon our departure I asked him what I owed, but his answer convinced me that his almost slavish hospitality gave the appearance but not the intention of being to my advantage. Therefore I lay that amount on the table so that everything was paid for in full.[4]

The 9th of March - To Sutte and Colenfelds in the district Blaumenau. On the way to these villages, at about nine o'clock in the morning, the captain, Lieutenant [Wilhelm Karl] von Donop, and I took leave until the following day, when the regiment did not march. The captain and Lieutenant von Donop went to Obernkirchen and I to Gattenburg, where I arrived at seven o'clock in the evening and met my brother. He was quite

****

4. The author provides a good description of how the officers were treated along the march route.

Bardeleben's Diary

healthy but rather unhappy or ill at ease, or maybe it is possible I misjudged. At least I can not be sure because my pleasure as well as his liveliness led to some excess. Our frantic efforts to obtain a horse put us in such a sweat that we had trouble dispelling the same. He was almost out of his mind. In short, I soon obtained a horse and did not feel bad about the inconvenience. However, all my persuasiveness had to be used to drive the feeling away. The postmaster in Rotenberg was away, the post horses were gone, and only his own were available. The postmaster's wife assured me that it was impossible to get a horse as all the city's inhabitants had sent theirs out to pasture, also. Now what, I thought. In this dilemma the brother of the postmaster arrived. He asked me the reason for my presence and said perhaps because of urgent reasons, in his opinion, good judgment made it necessary that I get it (his brother's horse) because the driver had just arrived from Obernkirchen, where he had picked up some mail. Once again joy and good feelings came over me and I made it my business to put the driver beside me in order to give him a feeling of importance and understandably to make that exceptional feeling an exceptional reward. My driver, on the other hand, swore that it was only from kindness and not from a feeling of obligation, that he rode with me. The long experience of his service had taught him to make detours with passengers such as I. I must say that I found in his conduct the greatest belief in his assurances. He drove like a madman, without avoiding holes or anything. In Katrinhagen, which neither of us knew the name of, because the driver was as unfamiliar with the way as I, he wanted a drink. Therefore, we stopped at an inn and drank, maybe somewhat more that we should have, because we were alone and it was cold. I did not believe a glass of spirits would make me confused, but that was the case. The beads of sweat and the small addition made a bad impression when I arrived in Cattenbruch. I was able to conceal my staggering actions. At the same time I thought that it could not remain unnoticed. The full-of-love behavior of my dear brother misled me into drinking more with him, and as a result I became really drunk. I pleaded a great tiredness and hurried off to bed.

The 10th of March - During the night my sleep was again sound but upon waking I only felt refreshed for fleeting moments as my conduct made me somewhat ashamed. Because my brother, as well as my oldest sister, who was also present, knew nothing of my yesterday's activities, I also kept silent. After we drank coffee, I rode in company with my brother, at eight o'clock, to Obernkirchen, where Captain [Christoph Dietrich von Donop] and Lieutenant von Donop arrived late at night and took lodgings in the house of Fraeulein von Donop. My brother and I dismounted there, paid our respects to Fraeulein von Gilsa, and went into the city with her to watch the von Lossberg Regiment march through.[5] During the afternoon the entire group ate at the home of the Cologne district administrator and when the meal was finished, we paid our compliments to the officers. At three o'clock in the afternoon we began our return. My driver, with whom I was fully satisfied and who just out of sociability put us up for the night at Cattenbruch, drove me on my way. I had to leave the other gentlemen outside the city because they were in no condition, with spent horses, to proceed to Rotenberg. Because my driver again drove like a well-behaved individual and in a manner to please me, I was happy. I had to travel the worst roads and most dangerous waterways, which could only be traveled quickly and successfully by the greatest skill. At ten o'clock in the evening I arrived in Lute, where Lieutenant Colonel [Karl Philipp] Heymell lay in quarters with his company and the von Kutzleben Company.

The 11th of March - To Heemaen, Rohrsen, and Gadesbuenden, in the district of Woellsse. I did not know what

****

5. The von Lossberg was another Hesse-Cassel regiment on the way to America.

to do here. Today we had a difficult route, but on the other hand, we had a great amount of food and drink.

The 12th of March - We crossed the Weser at Hoya, marched through the cities of Hoyerhagen, Duddenhausen, and Dedendorf. As we had to pass Eystrup, I took a short leave and briefly visited my brother. I found him, with his wife and her parents, to be in good health. After an hour visit, I followed the regiment again, and, on the road, joined Lieutenant Colonel Heymell, who, with his company, had to take quarters in Dedendorf. A captain of the Prussian service provided quarters for the lieutenant colonel and, instinctively, in looking back on the miserable houses here, the lieutenant colonel was kind enough to offer that I also take lodgings there. Although his house had limited space and did not appear to be the fanciest, he at once agreed and I gladly accepted. In this house everyone was as if with fellow farmers, or in part, made to feel comfortable. At least the good man could perhaps have had more money than influence. I can say nothing more definite about him because I was responsible for the wagons and engaged with the ordnance horses. The next morning I rode to Eystrup which lay about two and one-half miles from Dedendorf. Also, I could only judge from his overall impression and outward appearance. A few of the general's company, among others Captain [Friedrich Karl] von Weitershausen, had their quarters in Eystrup, and together with us had a day of rest. I visited him and Freyenhagen. We were pleased that a good ship's [?] had joined us during the entire march.[6]

****

6. I have been unable to decipher and translate a word at this point. I believe the author's meaning was that some type of vessel carrying necessities for sale to the soldiers accompanied the troops on the march to the sea.

Bardeleben's Diary

The 14th of March - To Kirchweyhe and Sudweyhe. At the latter the lieutenant colonel obtained his quarters with a noble official. That individual was not obligated to provide quarters, but because of politeness and a shortage of good quarters, he agreed to forego his rights. Therefore, he led his guests, despite having a separate residence, into his main residence, which certainly can be said to compare in splendor with a royal palace. The entire courtyard was surrounded by a great water-filled moat and provided with beautiful eye-catching carriage bridges. The lieutenant colonel was kind enough once again and took me with him. I then received the best of quarters and hospitality also. My room, provided with the best carpets and furniture, made a great impression on me. In short, I ate, drank, and slept like a prince. I have forgotten the noble's name.

The 15th of March - We crossed the Weser, passed through Bremen to Marsell, Burgdam, and Vorburgdam. Throughout this area the Weser had done much damage. In many places it had flooded and especially a few miles outside Bremen, near the village of Brinkum, which we had to pass, it had burst its dam so that the water poured over a paved section about two miles long. There the regiment had to be carried across, in part in small boats, and in part in wagons. Our march today was very difficult. At nine o'clock in the evening we finally reached our quarters, but lots of food and drink improved our dispositions.

The 16th of March - To Blumenthal, Ronnebeck, Beckedorff, and Vegesack. This latter place alone merits comment. Vegesack is only a small settlement. It has a rather spacious harbor in which twenty or thirty merchant ships can lie. It belongs to Bremen. The inhabitants of this small city appear to live in good circumstances. Lieutenant Colonel Heymell's Company and therefore, I also, was fortunately quartered in this place. I had lodgings with an apothecary by the name of Tillemann, a man whose attentiveness did everything which contributed to make my stay pleasant. His wife was no less involved and attentive and did everything possible for my comfort and to serve me. The food was exceptionally good and I can not remember having had any better. The politeness of these people went so far that because it was still rather cold, they even warmed my bed. My entrance into this situation, which was greatly improved with the finest bed and decorated with very fine blankets, would have satisfied a prince. I could not help but compare it with that of a nobleman, and I noticed the next morning that great difference from my usual practice in a similar situation. The service could not have been any better. I slept but little, and only because the bed was too good and seemed different to me. The private soldiers measure their life in the same way. They minimize the greatest good fortune and their whole life, which they have here for the first time. How can they think otherwise? Strong brandywine and beer would serve as their wine.

This good life continued until the seventeenth since we were fortunate enough to have a day of rest here. The overdone kindness of the apothecary told me because of his obvious embarrassment and many kindnesses, that I should not pay for fear that I would thus embarrass a man of consequence and believed nothing should be forced on him. Instead I sought to buy something of equal value as he had supplied everything for my entire provisioning on the ship's voyage. I also brought many of our officers to him so that they could buy their necessities from the man, and I had the best result in filling my intent. With the greatest joy he hugged me upon our departure as during these days he had more joy than in all of his years. I took the liberty to offer something, but this was his emotional answer, "Pay me for your indebtedness by giving an occasional thought to me."

The 18th of March - To Hagen, Kassebruch, and Driftsethe, in the district of Hagen. The pleasant must always be followed by the unpleasant, and in this manner first the true value must be determined. I even learned this here with full

Bardeleben's Diary

conviction. Misery and pain, thirst and hunger, are found everywhere. I had my quarters in Driftsethe. My host was an old man, whose only room seemed, by all indications, to be furnished comfortably. Pigs, geese, chickens, dogs, and cats, were his companions and all slept together in this room. And, furthermore, at night it became a smoky room, perhaps out of custom or necessity, even during my stay. This smoke had the effect to upset me, or at least by the next day to cause some smoked effect. Even though I opened the windows and doors, it was all in vain. The room was a sort of sleeping compartment, which was never meant to serve as an open area, but was a hole which my host and I had to share. The night was full of smoke and foul odors, and despite all that, I had to sleep therein. I acquired lots of fleas when I crawled in bed and they advanced against me so that all my defensive measures were not enough to drive them away. I killed herds of them but their numbers were unending. Later I slept quite well and gladly paid for my nights lodgings.

The 19th of March - To Stotel, Nesse, and Gackstadt. These were our cantonment quarters and from this time on our rations from Electoral Hannover subjects ceased. Every soldier had to pay for everything he consumed, and at rather high prices. The local farmers have been forced into such terrible circumstances for some years by an animal disease, that they have barely enough for their own needs. Some of the landed people have lost more than twenty cattle in a year and this also made food, especially meat, very scarce. Each noon meal cost the officers eight [groschen],[7] and still it did not taste good. Lieutenant Colonel Heymell's and the von Kutzleben Companies lay in [left blank]. A merchant by the name of Cammaron lives here, who served us our meals, also for eight groschen for a very good meal.

****

[7] The actual monetary units are at best an educated guess as the abbrerviations are impossible to decipher.

Bardeleben's Diary

I paid nothing during our entire stay, neither for food, nor drink. Lieutenant Colonel Heymell was good enough to give me everything possible free, even wine and coffee, because I did many favors, but I must confess that I did not do enough to earn all that his generosity extended to me. The friendly treatment by this individual made our entire stay very pleasant and held us together.

On the 30th of this month - We marched to be mustered not far from Bremerlehe, in a large courtyard, and at that place also took an oath of fidelity to the English Crown. His Excellency Lieutenant General [Leopold] von Heister and the English envoy Colonel von [sic - William] Faucitt were present. When this was finished we returned to our quarters. Otherwise nothing new occurred.

[In addition to the von Donop Regiment commanded by Lieutenant Colonel Heymell, the 1st Division of Hesse-Cassel troops contained of the officers and units in the following section:]

Names of the Generals of the 1st Division
Participating in the North American Campaign

1. Chief and Commander of the Corps of the 1st Division - Lieutenant General von Heister[8]

Brigade Commanders

1. Major General [Johann Daniel] Stirn
2. Major General [Martin] Schmidt
3. Major General [Werner] von Mirbach
4. Colonel [Friedrich Wilhelm] von Lossberg
5. Colonel [Karl Emil Ulrich] von Donop, Commander of all the grenadiers and jaegers.

****

8. The Hesse-Cassel troops saailed in two divisions, with the 1st Division sailing in two sections due to a shoratage of shipping.

Bardeleben's Diary

1st Division
Regimental Commanders

1. Grenadier Battalion von Linsing - Lieutenant Colonel [Otto Christian Wilhelm] von Linsing
2. Grenadier Battalion Block - Lieutenant Colonel [Justus Heinrich] Block
3. Grenadier Battalion von Minnigerode - Lieutenant Colonel [Friedrich Ludwig] von Minnigerode
4. Leib [Body] Regiment - Colonel [Friedrich Wilhelm] von Lossberg
5. Hereditary Prince Regiment - Colonel [Karl Wilhelm] von Hachenberg
6. Prince Charles Regiment - Colonel [Johann Wilhelm] Schreiber
7. Ditfurth Regiment - Colonel [Karl] von Bose
8. Donop Regiment - Colonel [David Ephriam] von Gose
9. Lossberg Regiment - Colonel [Henrich Anton] von Heringen
10. Knyphausen Regiment - Colonel [Heinrich] von Borck
11. Truembach Regiment - Colonel [Karl Ernst] von Bischhausen
12. Two Jaeger Companies - Colonel [Karl Emil Ulrich] von Donop
13. Two Artillery Companies - Lieutenant Colonel [Hans Heinrich] Eitel

The Grenadier Battalion von Linsing consists of the grenadier companies of the 2nd and 3rd Guards and the Leib and Mirbach Regiments.

The Grenadier Battalion Block consists of the grenadier companies of the Prince Charles, Wutginau [Landgraf], Donop, and Truembach Regiments.

The Grenadier Battalion von Minnigerode consists of the grenadier companies of the Hereditary Prince, Ditfurth, Lossberg, and Knyphausen Regiments.

Bardeleben's Diary

Names of the Officers of the von Donop Regiment Participating in the 1776 Campaign to North America

Rank and Name

1. Colonel Commandant von Gose
2. Lieutenant Colonel Heymell
3. Major [Erasmus Ernst] Hinte
4. Grenadier Captain von Weitershausen
5. Captain [Christian Moritz] von Kutzleben
6. Captain [Philipp Wilhelm[von Gall
7. Captain [No name entered - possibly Johann Matthias Gissot]
8. Captain [Justus Friedrich] Venator
9. Captain von Donop
10. 1st Lieutenant [Friedrich Wilhelm] Geisler
11. 1st Lieutenant [Philipp Heinrich] Murhard
12. 2nd Lieutenant [Emanual Rosinus] Hausmann
13. 2nd Lieutenant [Johann Philipp] Reiss (Grenadier)
14. 2nd Lieutenant von Nagel, Sr. [probably Heinrich Ludwig]
15. 2nd Lieutenant von Nagel [probably Karl Friedrich]
16. 2nd Lieutenant [Johann Heinrich] von Bardeleben
17. 2nd Lieutenant [Wilhelm] von Lepel
18. 2nd Lieutenant von Donop
19. 2nd Lieutenant [Karl August] Freyenhagen, Sr. (Grenadier)
20. Ensign [Jeremias] von Lossberg
21. Ensign [Eitel Wilhelm] von Trott
22. Ensign [Wilhelm Johann Ernst] Freyenhagen, Jr.
23. Ensign [Karl] von Knoblauch
24. Ensign [Franz Karl] von Stadell [or Staedell], died at sea on 22 June 1776
25. Regimental Quartermaster [Johann Georg] Zinn
26. Regimental Surgeon [Johann Jacob] Stiegelitz
27. Auditor [Bartholomai Ernst] Heymell
28. Chaplain [Georg Christian] Coester

Bardeleben's Diary

29. Wagonmaster [Daniel] Schultz

- - - - - - -

Grenadier Company strength   122 men
Musket Company strength   121 men
Plus their officers

- - - - - - -

On the ship *Hope*, Captain Peacock

1. Major Hinte, 2. Captain Venator, 3. Lieutenant Murhard, 4. Lieutenant Lepel, 5. Ensign von Lossberg, 6. Regimental Quartermaster Zinn, 7. Wagonmaster Schultz, the Major's Company and part of the Kutzleben Company

On the ship *Embres*, Captain Walles

1. Captain von Gall, 2. Lieutenant Hausmann, 3. Ensign Freyenhagen, 4. Lieutenant [Ernst Wilhelm] von Anderson of the Hereditary Prince Regiment, 5. Ensign [Reinhard Friedrich] Ungewitter of the Hereditary Prince Regiment, 121 men of the Leib Company, 35 men of the Hereditary Prince Regiment, and 18 men of the Lossberg Regiment - a total of 174 men

- - - - - - -

The 9th of April - Our regiment embarked on the Weser River near the village of Geestendorf, not far from Bremerlehe, and on the following ships:

On the ship *Esk*, Captain Redly

1. Colonel von Gose, 2. Captain von Donop, 3. Lieutenant von Nagel, Sr., 4. Lieutenant von Nagel, Jr., 5. Lieutenant von Donop, 6. Lieutenant Keyser of the Artillery, 7. Ensign von Stadell, 8. Regimental Surgeon Stiegelitz, 121 men of the Colonel von Gose Company, 43 men of the Captain von Kutzleben Company, and 12 men of the Artillery - a total of 176 men

Bardeleben's Diary

On the ship *Jenny*, Captain Hamilton

1. Lieutenant Colonel Heymell, 2. Captain Gissot, 3. Lieutenant von Bardeleben, 4. Ensign von Trott, 5. Ensign von Knoblauch, 6. Auditor Heymell, 7. Chaplain Coester, and 121 men of the company of Lieutenant Colonel Heymell, 34 men of the von Kutzleben Company, 20 men of the Lossberg Regiment, and 14 neb of the Artillery - a total of 189 men

- - - - - - -

By eleven o'clock in the morning we were on board our ships. What wonders, what amazement, and what thoughts I had as I went aboard ship! I, who had never imagined such a large ship, still less actually seen one, clearly experienced something that I was in no condition to evaluate. A silent wondering, a boundless astonishment, overtook me and dark images crossed my mind. In short, my ideas were too wild and too imperfect. I was understandably preoccupied trying to bring all my thoughts into a clear comprehension.

This is the place for a brief description of our cabin.

This cabin is not exceptionally large, about four paces long and equally as wide. It has four small windows and is otherwise equipped with equal decoration and comfort. So for example, there are four bedsteads therein, which quite fortunately are made according to the rules of need, and on the side, nailed fast, is a square table, which nearly fills the entire cabin; four wooden chairs, a stove, a large medicine chest, which is firmly tied to a bedstead, and in case of need, has to serve as a chamber pot, several portmanteau, which when necessary serve the same purpose. This especially chosen furniture was meant therefore for our comfort, and outside the room had very necessary decorations, five frightfully large hams hung outside the window in a row and nevertheless gave off a smell. On addition to these, twenty weapons lay above the hams, also a drum,. and finally,

Bardeleben's Diary

the wig of the pastor hung with other unending expensive things, according to the rank of each, and made the contrast complete.

It seems necessary and important enough to describe our diet here.

The following was given to us daily and each two to four pounds was enough for six men:

Monday - one-half pound of butter, one-half pound of cheese, two pounds of oatmeal, eight quarts of beer (four Maas), and four pounds of bread.

Tuesday - Four pounds of bread, eight quarts of beer, two pounds of fine wheat flour for pudding, and raisins, also one-half pound of beef.

Wednesday - Four pounds of bread, eight quarts of beer, one-half pound of butter, one-half pound of cheese, two pounds of oatmeal, and two pounds of peas.

Thursday - Bread, beer, two pounds of pork, and four pounds of peas.

Friday - Bread, beer, butter, cheese, oatmeal, and peas.

Saturday - Bread, beer, pudding with raisins, two pounds of beef.

Sunday - Beer, bread, pork, and peas.

From the tenth to the sixteenth of April all the ships lay peacefully at anchor on the Weser near Bremerlehe. Nothing of significance occurred for us during this time. On the eleventh of the month I wrote to Kassel to L. von G. and sent other letters with it. Just during these days we were visited by seven people. These were Captain Venator, Lieutenant Nagel, Sr., two Freyenhagens, Ensign von Lossberg, and two ship's captains, making with us, fifteen people - a real party. At the same time we were all in the cabin and had to take turns sitting on one another's lap, and patiently wait to see what we would get for food and drink. It is easily understood from the above comedy that everything tasted good to us and we toasted one another.

On the 16th of the month - Because a favorable wind arose, all the small boats were taken up and the anchor raised

Bardeleben's Diary

during the evening. The sails were unfurled so that on the following day we could depart for Portsmouth. His Excellence Lieutenant General von Heister therefore came aboard ship this afternoon and from most of the ships his departure was signalled with cannonfire.

The 17th of April 1776 - At eight o'clock in the morning all the ships set sail from Bremerlehe with a very good wind and exceptionally beautiful weather. The view of so many ships, about forty in number, was impressive. About eleven-thirty in the morning the land had almost disappeared and by three o'clock in the afternoon we left the Weser with the best wind and entered the North Sea, from which land could no longer be seen. From Bremerlehe to the North Sea the distance is seven German miles [42 English miles].[9] We covered this distance in a period of seven hours. From three o'clock this afternoon until six o'clock this evening, on almost all of the ships during such bright weather, the music of a continuous cannonfire. The splendor and pleasantness of this event can not be described. It is a situation which must be experienced to fully grasp. It was therefore a theater whose presentation caused the most wonderful reception of awe. The witness of each influenced against his will. At eight-thirty in the evening Helgoland was sighted, but at a great distance. The light from the lighthouse could barely be seen.

The 18th of April - This past night was our first night at sea. For me it was as peaceful as when on the Weser, but otherwise solid land called more and more. From yesterday at three o'clock in the afternoon until six o'clock this morning, we sailed 21 German miles [126 English miles]. Again the sky was generally clear and there was no wind. At eight-thirty in the

****

9. A German mile was equal to about six English miles and a German hour was equal to two and one-half English miles. Over a period of time the author seems to have gradually adopted the English mile as his unit of measure.

morning at a distance of about twelve English miles, the coast of East Friesland was seen. At this time the sea all about us was covered with East Friesland fishing boats. At eleven-thirty the wind became contrary, but until six o'clock in the evening the weather remained good and it was rather calm. Then it rained a little, but without becoming stormy. Most of the troops had to vomit violently today. However, I remained unaffected.

The 19th of April - Although our ship rolled rather unpleasantly during the night, I slept well and was unaware of it. Very pleasant weather and a wind calm, but no favorable wind. Almost all the soldiers were seasick and had to vomit whatever they could. Thank God, I still did not feel the least bit sick.

The 20th of April - I slept well during the past night. The weather was very pleasant again. The wind quite calm but not favorable. Therefore the ship made little headway and this was barely noticeable. At nine o'clock in the morning the sea was calm and no waves were visible. It was like sailing on a mirror. (These exceptionally smooth seas are called the sailors' calm.) At six o'clock in the evening innumerable fish, much like herring, were seen. These lay in great schools on the surface of the ocean, cavorting about. At seven o'clock in the evening the wind became favorable but was still so weak that the ship made very little headway. Almost no movement of the ship could be noticed during this calm. Seasickness continued just the same.

The 21st of April - Still healthy and the most pleasant sleep. The nice, bright, and calm weather continued with favorable but very weak wind. At three o'clock in the afternoon the wind blew somewhat stronger. At nine o'clock in the evening the wind became contrary, but still pleasant, good, and fine.

The 22nd of April - Quite fresh and healthy. The weather still very pleasant. The seas were smooth, but the wind contrary and weak so that the ship hardly moved. Today I went hunting. I shot two geese and four owls, otherwise nothing new.

Bardeleben's Diary

The 23rd of April - Today was no less pleasant than the previous one. The sea was calm and the wind contrary and quite weak so that in twelve hours we sailed barely one mile. At five o'clock in the evening the wind blew somewhat stronger and more favorably. The troops were a bit better.

The 24th of April - During the past night our ship, as we were told by the captain, supposedly rolled quite a bit, but my sleep was not light enough to be able to detect the movement. I certainly slept well enough. From yesterday at four o'clock in the afternoon until eight o'clock this morning our ship sailed 95 English miles and this wind continued just as favorable the entire day so that we sailed six and at times seven miles in an hour. At nine o'clock in the morning the coast of England was visible. It appeared to be white clouds. At twelve o'clock noon we left the North Sea and entered the [English] Channel near the city of Dover. The castle, like the city itself, appeared to be surrounded by white cliffs and was distinctly visible.

The 25th of April - The entire day was clear and the sea smooth, the wind contrary and very weak. At three o'clock in the afternoon, in the distance, at about nine or ten miles, the Isle of Wight could be seen, and at six o'clock in the evening, the ships at Spithead. We could have entered the harbor already today, but at six-thirty a strong wind sprang up which was against us. Therefore, at ten o'clock at night we anchored in the Channel, not far from the noted Isle of Wight.

The 26th of April - During the night the strong wind had abated. At five o'clock in the morning the anchor was raised and we sailed into the harbor. At seven o'clock we were close to the Portsmouth harbor, but because of the contrary wind, the entrance was very slow. Only at ten o'clock in the morning were we able to reach the roadstead at Spithead and fortunately, praise God, still healthy. Our ship's captain, who had spent eighteen years at sea, assured us that he could not recall such calm, peaceful, and pleasant weather on the ocean. He also felt

Bardeleben's Diary

fortunate without the least storm and with the very best weather to have sailed part of the frightful sea crossing.

The 27th of April - All our ships lay at anchor in the roadstead at Portsmouth. Many of the ships, occupied by English troops, which were to sail to America with us, also lay at anchor here. The location of our ships was very pleasant, lying between Portsmouth and the Isle of Wight, which provided the most splendid view. Everything was green, the weather beautiful, and everyone in good health.

The 28th of April -Still lying at anchor with good weather. Otherwise nothing new.

The 29th of April - All quiet, at anchor, cold and unfriendly weather, but no rain. Today those ships on which there were too many troops had some taken off and assigned on board other transport ships. From our regiment, four officers and 138 men were transferred to the ship *Surprise*. [Marginal note - Several of the ships received fresh provisions.]

From the ship *Esk* - Lieutenant von Nagel, Sr. and 34 men from Captain von Kutzleben's Company

From the ship *Jenny* - Ensign von Knoblauch and twenty men from Captain von Kutzleben's Company and twenty men from the von Lossberg Regiment

From the ship *Hope* - Captain Venator and 34 men from Captain von Kutzleben's Company

From the ship *Embres* - Thirty men from the Leib Company of our regiment and the Lossberg Regiment

Therefore the occupants of the ship *Surprise* were: 1) Captain Venator, 2) Lieutenant von Nagel, Sr., 3) Lieutenant von Nagel, Jr., 4) Ensign von Knoblauch, and 5) 138 non-commissioned officers and privates.

The 30th of April - Very raw and cold weather with some rain. All the ships still lay at anchor. Nothing more new.

Bardeleben Diary

The 1st of May - Fair weather. Everyone still at anchor. At nine o'clock this morning I went into Portsmouth with the ship's captain. This city is of moderate size, surrounded by a wall, and strongly fortified with cannons on the side toward the sea. This city is also pleasantly situated and the entire area appears to be fertile. The streets are rather broad and well-paved. One in particular is exceptionally long and goes from one end of the city to the other. Half of the city has individual but very low-built houses. The other half, which is cut off by a water, and which is reached by crossing a stone bridge to the opposite shore, is nicer and the houses are much larger. Cleanliness, by which each is maintained, makes the houses attractive and splendid. The harbor is large and a wharf built alongside can be used to build ships as well as to repair ships of all types with the greatest ease. This wharf also has a deep brick-lined channel leading to a lock filled with water, which can be drained. This allows the ships to come in or to go out. Two of the warships, ready for sailing, each of ninety cannons, called the *Centaur* and the *Terrible*, were repaired here. The size of a warship is astonishing and it is impossible to look into the depth of one without shuddering. The cabins are large, among others, one in which there is room enough for about twenty men (four such cabins on each ship). Above all, Portsmouth is well and advantageously situated for handling ships. The warehouses are well-supplied with everything necessary for shipping concerns. Everything here was terribly expensive, for instance, coffee costs 16 to 20 groschen, a bottle of wine, 24 groschen, etc. I have been in the city of Gosport, also, which lies on the other side of the harbor from Portsmouth, but saw it only from one side. It also appears to be about the same size as Portsmouth. I returned aboard ship at five o'clock in the evening.

The 2nd of May - Unfriendly and cold weather. Still at anchor. Nothing new.

The 3rd of May - At ten o'clock in the morning all the ships sailed from Spithead to St. Helens in order to run out with the first good wind. At twelve o'clock noon the anchor was dropped and we lay one-half mile from the Isle of Wight. As much as I wanted to go onto this island, the stormy waves prevented it. The weather was cold and stormy.

The 4th of May - Stormy weather and cold. Everyone at anchor off St. Helens. Some departure! This afternoon one of Lieutenant Colonel Heymell's servants came aboard our ship to report to the colonel that one of his horses had been killed by another. This servant asked the sailors who had brought him to tie their boat alongside until his errand was completed. They did this and during this period spent their time in the cabin of our sailors. Soon the waves beat so strongly against their boat that the rope broke and suddenly it was driven so far away that it appeared impossible to recover. A sailor on another ship saw the boat and, making a quick decision, jumped into the water, followed it, caught it, and brought it again to our ship. For more than a quarter-hour he fought against the monstrous waves. It was frightening to watch how this man was violently thrown about by the waves. Often he could not be seen for two or three minutes, despite his efforts. He refused to accept money from the lieutenant colonel and absolutely refused it.

The 5th of May - At anchor off St. Helens. The storm waves continued so strong and without let-up. The waves nearly rolled over our ship and mounted until they appeared similar to snow-covered hills. At the same time there was hail, it rained, and at certain times, there was sunshine. In short, it was like a day in April. The ship made some maneuvers and brought us to our assigned place, of which we had not been completely certain. Our attentiveness continued. Toward evening the ship's cabin boys entered and said all chests and all cases, in fact everything that could be filled, should be taken out. We thought, what is the meaning of this? We soon noticed, however, that it was difficult for us to stand steady. We were soon reconciled to our staggering back and forth and realized the reason for the cabin boys' warning. Later we were pleased to have made the preparations but could not totally grasp why everything so terrible had to be connected with the sailors.

The 6th of May - During the past night the stormy weather abated and became quite good. We also had a good wind. We departed from St. Helens and sailed with the best northwesterly wind at six o'clock, convoyed by three warships, two frigates, and one bombship, three galleys and one fireship. At Portsmouth there were still some transport ships with English troops, which came out and joined us. Our fleet consisted then of seven warships and eighty transport ships, under the command of Commodore Sir [William] Hotham, who was on board the *Preston*.

The 7th of May - During the past night a strong wind again arose and the movement of the ship was unpleasant, although I slept well. At seven o'clock in the morning the wind was still strong and again contrary so that we had to sail back to St. Helens and await the coming of day. With this strong wind all the ships tacked with the greatest care so that they should not ground in the Channel. This special maneuvering by the ships caused nearly all of the troops such a feeling of sickness that they could not prevent vomiting and everything connected therewith. At six o'clock in the evening the waves rose much higher. No one could stand or even sit. We lay down therefore, part in bed, part on the bare floor, but we were still not secure. Soon the tables and chairs flew together, although they had been tied, which helped but little, and we were in the midst of them. We had our noon meal in great discomfort. One took his plate in bed, the next one sat down under the bed, and still another sat in the middle of the cabin and wrapped his arms around the table. In this manner we ate our meal. I sat on the deck beside my bed, holding onto it, ate some from a wooden bowl and accepted an incomparable taste. Now we understood how necessary it was to tie everything as tight as possible.

The 8th of May - The strong wind abated during the night and blew more favorably. Also, the weather turned quite nice.

Bardeleben Diary

The troops recovered once again. This morning we sailed very swiftly, eight English miles an hour. We ran along the English coast. At four o'clock in the afternoon we passed Plymouth at no great distance. It was possible to see the church spires of the city with the aid of a telescope. During the evening the weather raged intermittently and at any moment, just as on the previous day, the troops began to vomit again.

The 9th of May - Beautiful weather. The wind again soft and also favorable. At eleven o'clock in the morning we left the Channel and, praise God, safely. As long as we were still in the Channel our ship's crew had to sail no less carefully because the dangerous sandbanks can make this region of the coast difficult to travel. Throughout the day we sailed four, five, and even six English miles in an hour.

The 10th of May - Uncommonly good weather and wind and the sea calm. The sea was smooth as a mirror. The troops recovered somewhat. We sailed slowly, hardly two English miles in an hour.

The 11th of May - Still so slow, but beautiful, pleasant weather. The wind calm and the sea as smooth as yesterday. All day today we sailed only a few English miles.

The 12th of May - The same nice weather. Nothing more pleasant, nothing more splendid to imagine than such incomparably wonderful weather at sea.

The 13th of May - Still such good weather but with a bit more wind. Our voyage still made little headway. At seven o'clock in the evening the wind became more favorable and we traveled three to four English miles in an hour.

The 14th of May - Really good weather but cold air. The wind so favorable that we sailed five to six English miles in an hour.

The 15th of May - Fair weather. Raw air. The wind was still very good and we continued to sail as swiftly as yesterday, six to seven English miles an hour.

Bardeleben Diary

The 16th of May - Still reasonably good weather. Still cold. The wind still as desired and every hour we sailed six to seven English miles. Although the wind was not strong, the sea was so rough that our ship plunged first forward and then sideways and today we also lurched about in the cabin like a bunch of drunks. We were thrown from one corner to the other. We tied our coffeepot on a line this morning and fastened it on a nail where everyone put it to use and held his cup to be filled with unsteady hands and feet. It was no better with our noon meal. We had to put things together around the table and ate on the cabin floor while the servants, with the help of the table, held silverware and dishes. Under these conditions each helped the other as best he could. All this unpleasantness shook us a great deal. At least for my part I continued to eat and drink just as much as before, and the idea of not eating at sea until full, was for me, a measure of meaningless warning. I kept my appetite for food and drink at all times and at noon and in the evening ate the usual portion.[10]

The 17th of May - During the past night all of us slept very restlessly. The waves beat against the ship and due to their rapid movement, caused such severe rolling that at midnight all the chairs, books, valises, and even Captain Gissot, flew about in the cabin, and of all the things in the cabin, not much was spared. I myself nearly had the same fate when I was caught in the first tumult. I held on as tightly as possible and heard thereby the various events which occurred. Suddenly one of the other officers awoke, "Well!" he shouted. Then another, "Well what's happening?" The puzzle soon solved itself. One severe rocking of the ship followed after another, and suddenly such a jolt struck, that it nearly threw Captain Gissot out of bed. At the

****

10. The author is referring to the belief that if a person eats only light meals he will not get seasick.

same time, and just at that moment, everything was a cause of alarm. I lay absolutely quiet, said nothing, and acted as if asleep, but I thought to myself, Heavens! There is no storm but still such a dreadful rolling. A secret shudder seized me as I have never heard of such rolling, still less felt the same. I believed nothing more than that the ship would sink. I remained in this anticipation until daybreak, when it abated. We then got up, praise God, and told each other our many anxieties. Fair weather, raw and still favorable wind.

The 18th of May - The past night was somewhat more restful. Our ship made no little movement but nothing as severe as on the sixteenth and seventeenth. The air still raw. The wind was excellent and we sailed just as swiftly as on the previous day.

A young lad from the ship's crew, of about eleven years of age, fell from the lowest part of the mast, into the sea, this morning at six o'clock. The ship's captain had the small boat lowered immediately, went after him, and found him after he had been swimming around for twenty minutes. He was still alive and had all the life signs.

The 19th of May - The night was peaceful. We slept well. Good weather. The wind still very favorable. The young boy was already on deck again today and almost completely recovered.

The 20th of May - Wind, weather, and journey were good during the morning. At twelve o'clock noon it became so calm that we barely traveled one English mile in an hour, and this continued all day. The wind was contrary.

The 21st of May - The night was very restless. The back and forth rocking of our ship was very violent so that when we awoke in the morning, books, hams, chairs, and everything similar, was scattered about the cabin. This violent rocking was not caused by the wind, because it had hardly blown during the night, and even this morning was almost calm. The constant restlessness of the ocean alone caused the rocking. At twelve

Bardeleben Diary

o'clock noon, around the horizon it was overcast and a strong north wind arose so quickly that we believed the strongest storm was upon us. The waves rose so high at this time that they beat over our ship with the greatest force. The wind was also terrible and this weather continued the whole day. Our ship's crew did not consider it a storm, but for us it was one of the strongest because at noon today we could only eat or drink less serenely than usual. Our meal was very scant, only a pudding, but it could not be eaten peacefully. When it was placed on the table, it fell out of the wooden serving dish, rolled about on the table, and nearly fell on the floor. However, because all of us, as we were accustomed to doing, had previously situated ourselves advantageously, we were quick enough to catch it again. This pudding stayed on the table, completely clean, but it was in numerous small pieces. This could not be prevented because one hastily grabbed it with a fork to keep it from falling on the floor. Another used two or three knives, the third with a spoon, and the fourth with only his ten fingers. We were happy however, that we had been able to save it. The small pieces tasted just as good to us and nothing remained afterward.

The 22nd of May - Once again sleep was very restless. The stormy weather continued throughout the night without let-up and also just as severe as today. The ocean raged frightfully and the crashing was fierce and frightening. Monstrous waves beat against the ship and with such force that we believed the constant creaking of the masts must soon lead to our sinking. At eleven o'clock noon the strength of the storm increased. Almost no one could then remain on deck. All the food flew off the stove and lay scattered about. It was peas and ham. Therefore this afternoon we had nothing to eat but cheese and bread. We lay down in bed with this and ate our little bit with pleasure. We had tied a small cask with beer to the stove and this beneficial drink satisfied us very well. Toward evening the wind abated but only a little.

Bardeleben Diary

The 23rd of May - The past night was a bit more peaceful. The violent rolling, however, began again this morning, even stronger than on the previous day. It was very dark during the whole morning. The howling of the wind and waves, mixed together, threatened us with a sad day. Our dinner again consisted of bread and cheese. At two o'clock in the afternoon the stormy weather abated and the weather improved. How this pleasant change pleased us and how eagerly we hurried to cook. Each one on this evening wanted that which for the past several days was denied his stomach. During the past night the wife of one of the soldiers went into labor and fortunately delivered a fine son. The child was healthy but the mother very weak.

The 24th of May - The night was quite restful. During the day very good and pleasant weather and almost calm. The wind not favorable. We made little headway. At three o'clock in the afternoon the child was baptized. Lieutenant Colonel Heymell, our ship's captain, and Mr. Ego were the godparents. The lieutenant colonel held for the christening. He was named Carl for the lieutenant colonel, Hamilton for the ship's captain, and Heinrich, my name. The mother was already much better today.

The 30th of May - This is the first time in five days that I can take up my pen and I am glad that I am able to do so. A storm, a real storm, which struck at twelve o'clock noon on the 25th, did not allow us the least opportunity to write. Those days were exceptionally frightful, from the 25th to the 29th. We had to tolerate the most violent sea storm for varying degrees during this time, and none of the other various storms could compare with this storm. The west wind blew constantly so that we had the ever-present fear of losing our masts, or even losing the ship. My pen is too weak, the language is too poor, to fully describe all the danger. Here the waves could hardly be called hills any longer, but seemed to be monstrous, even incalculably high mountains. Wave after wave rolled and raged against one another in the dreadful crashing.

Bardeleben Diary

The waves often covered our entire ship so that the water was two or three feet deep on the deck. Therefore no one dared to go on deck without risking his life if hit by a wave. Even our ship's crew had difficulty to stand. When they stood on the helm, they had to be tied to the mast. From five to six o'clock on the 28th our danger was greatest. The waves surrounded us on all sides. Our ship seemed to lie at the bottom of the deepest pit. The water beat against the hatches and flowed from the deck into our cabin like a stream. The lieutenant colonel, who had stood up so that his bed could be made and only held firmly onto the door of his cabin while this was done, was struck by a wave which beat over this place with its full fury during this hour, and so drenched him that he came into our cabin thoroughly soaked. This same wave also hit me. Hunger had driven me from my bed, which I crawled out of with great effort. I sat on the deck near a cabinet in order to get a bit of bread and cheese. However, I had barely opened the cabinet when the water came in through the stove pipe and struck my leg. At this moment the lieutenant colonel, and shortly thereafter the ship's captain, entered the cabin no less dejected and ill at ease. At this moment everything was in disarray. We were a sad sight to one another and fearfully awaited the moment when we would become the victims of this wild flood. We could not shut our eyes during this entire period, and if we rested a little, it was a fitful sleep that weakened more than refreshed us. Despite all this, the new mother and her child, without anxiety or fear, spent these terrible days in the best of health. May the Lord be eternally praised for our rescue and the most fortunate survival of all the dangers which we had to face. During this entire day very pleasant weather. What a chance for us to quickly recover, as we had barely seen the light of day for five days. Each one crawled feebly out, weakly looked about to ascertain if the frightful theater of nature, of fear and grief, had really passed. Everyone then breathed with eager gasps the soft air and everyone was gradually stimulated from his almost completely exhausted spirit to display a bit more liveliness. The commodore aboard the *Preston* made a signal early this morning that all the ship's captains were to come to him in order to learn if any misfortunes had occurred. However, the fleet was so scattered that he could get these reports from only a few ships. The ships gradually drew together and almost all had been lucky. A few had lost masts.

The 31st of May - The past night was the first in the last six days during which we could really enjoy our rest. Exceptionally good and bright weather but no favorable wind. At noon it was absolutely necessary, as we had not yet recovered and the gentlemen could get out of the cabin, to get at least a little proper rest. We hurried with hugh appetites to our noonday meal but there was nothing to enjoy. The whole meal had acquired the most unpleasant smell for the water in which it had been cooked. We had to take simple bread and cheese in preference. This incident happens often because the water, above all, is terrible and almost stinks, and is so scarce that no one is allowed to wash his hands or face, except with seawater. Even when the water becomes contaminated it has to serve.

NB - Coffee and tea are enjoyed if the smell is only mildly bad.

Bardeleben Diary

The 1st of June - The previous night was quite peaceful. Slept very well. Early morning was dull and foggy. Almost calm and no good wind. At nine o'clock in the morning it was generally clear and the weather excellent. At six o'clock in the evening a heavy fog set in and persisted. The wind blew rather strong. It was learned this morning that the ship *Malaga*, on which were Captain [Peter Michael] Waldenberger with his company of the Leib Regiment, had strayed from the fleet during the last storm and we could not learn what had happened to it.

The 2nd of June - The night was quiet. Slept well. Very healthy. Very nice weather, but terribly hot. The wind however, calm. We made little headway. This morning we received 45 bottles of porter beer from our ship's captain, but did not divide it among us. Instead, all of it was given to me and each one had the privilege, according to his desire, to drink a little or a lot, and what his pocketbook permitted.

The 3rd of June - The night was very peaceful. Slept really well. A great heat all day. No wind and calm. We hardly moved.

The 4th of June - Today was not as nice as the previous ones, brighter but cold air. The sea rather restless but the rolling of the ship was not severe. We could eat and drink in peace. Contrary wind. At ten o'clock in the morning Lieutenant General von Heister visited the commodore on board the *Preston* to help celebrate the birthday of the King of England. Therefore during the noon time a strong salute was fired by the war and transport ships.

The 5th of June - The sea peaceful. The wind not strong but contrary. It rained almost all day, otherwise nothing new.

The 6th of June - The morning was overcast and foggy. The air cold and still a contrary wind. At noon clear and bright weather. However, we made little headway, barely two or three English miles in an hour. A French ship bound for America was stopped today and then had to remain by the fleet. During the afternoon Captain Venator and Lieutenant von Nagel, Sr. visited

Bardeleben Diary

us in order to buy sugar and other foodstuffs from our ship's captain, because for a long time already they have had nothing but ship's provisions.

The 7th of June - The weather was dreary all day and sunshine alternated with rain. No good wind. We made little headway.

The 8th of June - The weather was rather clear. Cold air. The wind still contrary. We made little headway.

The 9th of June - Excellent weather. Very hot. No wind and calm.

The 10th of June - Rather good weather. The wind somewhat better and stronger. However, we made little headway.

The 11th of June - Stormy weather. The sea very restless and it rained until evening. The wind contrary. Our noon meal was eaten with great difficulty. We had dumplings made from flour, crushed ship's zwieback, and a bit of suet, with water stirred in. They tasted good. A large wooden bowl was well-filled and while we were not allowed to have plates because of the ship's rolling, all of us ate out of this single bowl which one of us held tight.

The 12th of June - The same weather as yesterday. As a result we could not eat comfortably again, which was healthy and, praise God, nothing was needed. Bread, cheese, and beer were for us excellent.

The 13th of June - The stormy weather partially abated and again was rather good. The wind somewhat better. At four o'clock in the afternoon we saw many large fish which were about twelve feet long. However, no one knew their name.

The 14th of June - According to talk among the officers, our ship rolled violently during the past night. For my part, however, when I awoke I knew nothing about it. Good weather all day and calm. Although our ship danced about a lot, we made little headway. Such movement often occurs when the ocean surface is smooth. The constant restlessness of the sea is the cause of the movement. We learned the bad news today that Captain [Simon Ludwig Wilhelm], Count von der Lippe and Lieutenant [Karl August] Kleinschmidt, both of the Leib Regiment, fought a duel aboard ship on the sixth of this month. The Count was mortally wounded and died soon thereafter of his wound. [Marginal note - after two days] Lieutenant Kleinschmidt was taken on board Colonel [Friedrich Wilhelm] von Wurmb's ship as a prisoner.

The 15th of June - The night rather peaceful. The weather variable - first rain and then sunshine; first strong wind and then light wind. Very cold. At noon more tolerable and better, the wind more favorable. We sailed three or four English miles in an hour. During the evening a gigantic ship was seen which according to the ship's captain could be as much as 800 tons.

The 16th of June - The weather rather bright but as cold as in October. We sailed along like yesterday. We ate our noon meal in complete peace. We had a good soup made with chicken, twelve of which the lieutenant colonel had brought aboard ship. Wonderful pork, pudding, and cheese tasted good.

The 17th of June - Exceptionally nice weather. Very hot. No wind at all and calm. During the afternoon we had a visit. Major Hinte, Captain [Adam Christoph] Steding of the von Lossberg Regiment, Chaplain Heller, and two ship's captains. A pleasant day. We enjoyed the time drinking punch, a bit too much, and a very innocent gaiety prevailed. At seven o'clock in the evening the visitors departed.

The 18th of June - Incomparable weather. We sailed three or four miles per hour. Today I did not feel well. Perhaps too much yesterday. Nevertheless, I still ate well. We had dumplings.

The 19th of June - Good weather. Very hot. Wind fair and we sailed at three miles per hour. Today I again felt better.

The 20th of June - Quite bright during the morning and good weather. During the afternoon so foggy that it was nearly impossible to see another ship. Still, we sailed as swiftly as yesterday.

The 21st of June - The fog which set in yesterday afternoon continued all day today and still so thick that no other ship could be seen. Our ship's captain therefore was greatly embarrassed, the more so because he no longer heard the fireship which the commodore sent every hour with reports and to check the course. He believed we were at a great distance from the fleet. Nevertheless, we sailed on and luckily, at five o'clock in the evening, as it began to brighten, we found ourselves near the commodore's ship. At seven o'clock in the evening a few other ships could be seen. Late in the evening it began to rain very hard and suddenly the fog set in again. At nine o'clock in the evening we drank a fine punch.

The 22nd of June - The fog which had continued for two days completely vanished at five o'clock this evening. The weather was rainy from the previous night continuously until two o'clock in the morning. Rather clear but so cold that we would like to have seen a warm stove. After the fog our fleet was very small; it had been completely scattered and only now and then was a ship to be seen. The commodore often fired [cannon shots] so that those still far away could hear and determine their location. Our ship was one of the first to join the commodore. The others hurried back. Today our ship's captain took a sounding and found bottom at seventy fathoms. We also noticed that we had found the Sable Bank. All sorts of fish and birds were to be seen in great numbers. We saw fish the size of which was noteworthy. The crew called them fin-fish and estimated them to be 700 to 800 pounds, but inedible.[11]

The 23rd of June - Very foggy all day and cold; so thick during the evening that no ship was visible to another. Our ship's captain threw out fish lines and caught three fish, each one

****

11. Fin fish are fin whales.

fifteen to eighteen pounds. They are called kabbeljaws and labretans.[12] We ate one this evening with a sauce made of melted butter and a little flour. It tasted very good.

The 24th of June - The fog persisted all day just as thick as yesterday. No ships were visible but in the distance ships' bells could be heard. The fog really settled in and seemed without end. However, the sea was peaceful and almost calm. We tried again today to catch fish but could not find bottom. At noon, however, while eating our lunch, someone came into the cabin and in a loud voice shouted, "Look how many fish!" We left our dinner and everything else and hurried on deck. An innumerable great many fish completely surrounded our ship, as far as could be seen. A host of them were swimming among one another. We could not learn what they are called but they were very large, almost ten feet long. Above all the variety and number of marine animals is beyond belief and even the smallest species shows the greatness of the Creator.

The 25th of June - Exceptionally bright and clear weather. Absolutely no wind and calm. We were no longer on the Sable Bank.

The 26th of June - Good weather almost all day. The sky was very bright. No wind and almost calm. At five o'clock in the evening fog set in again, but not too thick nor persistent. Late in the evening the weather cleared again. Our ship's captain gave us 48 bottles of porter beer today, eight bottles for each.

The 27th of June - Pleasant weather, but rather windy although not rough. Wind, sea, and everything else, even us in the cabin, were peaceful, but no wonder. At noon and again at night we had time to eat, but our anticipation fooled us. At twelve o'clock everything was quiet, but still no food and we did not even know that none would be delivered.

****

12. These are cod fish.

Bardeleben Diary

Finally, because we had waited so long, we went in and confronted the people in the kitchen to bring us some food. What an answer we received. Only a small piece of pork cooked in seawater. Everything else had been eaten. Now what? Someone gave this advice, the next something else, the third sighed, and the others complained. In short it was decided to put buckwheat gruel on the stove. It was cooked, rather thick, and in short order. Buckwheat and pork became our noon meal. This prank was frequently played on us and for some time has often been our dinner and attended with some difficulty. Our cook, Captain-at-arms [Georg] Wehrmann of Colonel Block's Company, had been sick and could not fulfill his duties. Therefore our ship's rations were given first to the ship's cook, then to my batman, and then again to the captain-at-arms or to his wife. This often resulted in errors. I was responsible for providing the person to do the cooking and often forgot to ask who could cook for us and what he was to cook. As a result, like today, we had to suffer. We learned that several ships, including Colonel Block's, had become separated from the fleet during the last fog.

The 28th of June - At four o'clock in the morning Pastor Coester and I arose, went on deck, and watched the splendid rising sun. Excellent weather all day. Warm, no wind and calm. At five o'clock in the evening a favorable wind arose and we sailed six English miles in an hour. This afternoon we were guests of the ship's captain. We had a pastry of fresh pork which he had received as a gift from one of his friends yesterday. He prepared it as follows: He made a dough with flour and water and brandy mixed together in a culinary style. The dough was then cut in large sheets and part laid underneath in the Cahtrol.[13] On top of that, the pork plus some beef, both cut into very small pieces, and again some of the dough, and so on.

****

13. Possibly I have misread the spelling of this word as I can not find it in either German or English dictionaries.

Then a sauce of flour, butter, water, and many spices was cooked and finally all this together was eaten with relish. It tasted good. Almost the entire day today was spent eating and drinking. While we drank our coffee, the ship's captain went out on deck and as one of his friends was sailing past us, closely, called to him through a megaphone, that he had fresh pork. If the friend were hungry, he was invited to share. The friend came immediately, drank coffee with us too, and then punch was made and the fresh meat roasted on the fire. Everyone ate again with such good appetites that we almost became sick.

The 29th of June - Rather good weather but the wind no longer favorable, although we sailed two or three miles an hour. Late in the evening the sea was a bit rough and thin fog set in. The movement of the ship became unpleasant and gave us a restless night.

The 30th of June - Despite yesterday's stormy weather, which continued during the past night and caused the ship to rock violently, the night was completely restful for me. The other officers assured me, however, that they were able to enjoy very little rest. The wind and sea were still rather restless although we were still able to hold religious services. We sailed more rapidly during the evening, reaching five, six, and seven miles an hour.

Monday, the 1st of July - During the past night our ship made such violent movements that it awakened all of us. This back and forth rocking was only caused, however, by a very good east wind, which sprang up at midnight. It drove our ship so far ahead of the fleet that we had to take in more sails and we nearly remained still until the others caught the same wind. Wind and weather were very good. We sailed a steady six miles an hour.

Tuesday, the 2nd of July - Very quiet during the past night. From this morning until three o'clock in the afternoon the best weather. Thereafter a heavy fog set in and no other ships

Bardeleben Diary

were visible. The wind still favorable, but because it was weak, we made little headway, about two miles an hour.

Wednesday, the 3rd of July - The wind still good. The fog continued all day and no ships could be seen, although we were lucky enough to remain near the commodore and every hour could hear the cannon fire. At six o'clock in the evening the fog cleared and it became completely calm. However, at ten o'clock the fog set in again. At four o'clock in the afternoon the fleet changed direction because it was believed to be too near the coast of Halifax. Thereafter the fleet turned out to sea.

Thursday, the 4th of July - Wind and sea rather peaceful and almost calm, but considerable fog alternating with sunshine. This weather lasted all day. The fog became heavier and seemed endless.

Friday, the 5th of July - Wind and sea pleasant. The fog continued until three o'clock in the afternoon, when the weather became quite clear. We sailed smoothly but instead of sailing forward, we sailed about thirty miles in the opposite direction. At nine o'clock in the evening it lightninged.

Saturday, the 6th of July - It rained during the morning. The sea was restless. The wind fair and we sailed well. At noon the best of weather, everything clear and the air fresh. What a joy it would have been to have seen land this afternoon. Everyone was filled with expectation; everyone kept looking all around and believed at any moment to catch sight of a strip of land through the mist. Our imagination was heightened because on all the ships, even our own, the sailors sat on the masts, hoping to see land, also. The fog had fooled all of us and suddenly all our joy disappeared. "But wait until tomorrow!" the soldiers said. "Then we will surely see land!" I wished this along with them, not for my sake alone, but more in consideration for the soldiers, who no longer knew how to tolerate the itch and rash.

Sunday, the 7th of July - Yesterday's longings were not in vain. We saw land. I was the first to see it. Early, before

Bardeleben Diary

daybreak, one of our sailors came to the cabin to awaken me and give me the news. I hurried on deck at once, looked around, but could see nothing. Shortly however, I discovered a bit of land. After the sun rose at three-thirty it was clearly visible and I informed everyone about it. They all ran out on deck. We drew steadily closer to the land. It was the coast of America, which at first glance had the appearance of clouds and at the same time looked like a distant, and to us, extensive China. At noon we could see the coast very distinctly and even see the [light] tower at which point we were eighteen [English] miles from Halifax. This tower is built [Marginal Note - very high and] on a cliff. It serves to warn ships away from the coast, which to the left and right consists of rocky cliffs, and to facilitate the entrance to Halifax harbor.

We sailed to the right, which was the way to Halifax, and saw some warships, here awaiting ours. We felt certain now that we would be put ashore and the soldiers had to fix their equipment. [Code - The lieutenant colonel thought the rebels would kill us at once. He thought that there would be a major battle fought today.] However, about four or five miles from Halifax, the admiral made a signal for all ship's captains to report to him. Here they were told that our destination was not Halifax, but Rhode Island, still 500 miles away. The ships, eighteen in number, which had become separated from the fleet a week ago, had been in the harbor at Halifax for two days and now rejoined us again, except the *Surprise* was not present and no one knew anything about it. *Malaga* had captured a small American ship and also rejoined us here. Now we were ready to sail from this island, but this was also denied. At three o'clock in the afternoon a frigate entered with the admiral's order and all the ship's captains were immediately ordered to report aboard the admiral's ship. It concerned a change in our sailing orders and New York was given as our destination. All our joy therefore soon turned to misery and we departed in sorrow. We had good weather all day and calm. The wind was not favorable and we made little headway.

Monday, the 8th of July - Initially foggy. Otherwise nothing new.

Tuesday, the 9th of July - Pleasant weather all day with light wind, almost calm. The fireship *Strombolo* collided with a transport ship during the afternoon so that these two ships hung together more than half an hour and caused great excitement. *Strombolo* lost the bowsprit but otherwise had no damage.

Wednesday the 10th of July - Dreary weather. At five o'clock in the afternoon the wind and the sea became very restless. The cabin boy came to us hurriedly and said we should secure everything in the cabin. It appeared that we would have a storm. However, the threatening weather passed and at eight o'clock in the evening it was quiet, peaceful, and almost calm. We made little headway.

Thursday, the 11th of July - The weather was very gloomy. Exceptionally foggy. At four o'clock in the afternoon it was almost clear but a few hours later a thick fog covered the sea and not another ship could be seen. The wind was quiet and calm. At nine o'clock in the evening we had a nature scene which we had not had before. A strong and frightful electrical storm struck. The crash of thunder was accompanied by the most terrible lightning so that it often seemed that fire, water, and ship were a single object. The rain fell like a torrential rain. This weather continued without let-up and in the strongest manner until one o'clock at night. Our ship lost a mast. Our ship's crew assured us that they could not remember ever experiencing such weather before. Today we began to reduce the beer. Where before we drank twenty bottles, we now had only nine bottles. We accepted the reduction against our will in order to make this beneficial drink last longer. The soldiers have been without this already for three weeks and have had to drink only rum mixed with water.

Bardeleben Diary

Friday, the 12th of July - Wind and sea very restless and otherwise bright weather with no clouds in the sky.

Saturday, the 13th of July - The wind and sea became less restless during the past night and the whole day was bright and peaceful.

Sunday, the 14th of July - Everything still and peaceful but overhead dark and overcast. It rained during the afternoon but not very long. At four o'clock in the afternoon rather bright and calm. At six o'clock in the evening a thick fog set in and continued. Very hot. It thundered and lightninged but at a great distance and only a little. Late in the evening it rained heavily. At six o'clock in the evening a great disturbance occurred on our ship. A transport ship came so close to ours that on both sides every effort was made so at least not to come together too hard. Both ships took such fortunate action that neither hit the other. Only by a small degree was our cabin spared from damage because just behind it the other ship had approached and the bowsprit extended nearly to our rigging. These collisions, when one ship rams another, are not rare during calm and fog and occur almost daily. Major Hinte's ship, among others, suffered much damage and nearly sank. This happened in Portsmouth as we lay at anchor, when a fireship tore loose from its anchor and crashed into his ship, so hard that all the lines from the forward part of the ship tore loose. The ship also suffered large holes in several places.

Monday, the 15th of July - The wind was not strong but the sea was high and the movement of the ship rather great. We made little headway.

Tuesday, the 16th of July - The weather agreeable. Wind and sea peaceful and almost calm. Chaplain Coester, our ship's captain, and I went aboard the ship *Hope* this morning to visit the major. Everything went well and pleasantly. After dinner a child was baptized. The wife of one of the major's soldiers had delivered a son. We then drank coffee and punch and departed again at six in the evening.

Bardeleben Diary

Wednesday, the 17th of July - Exceptionally beautiful weather all day. The wind unfavorable and we made little headway.

Thursday, the 18th of July - Incomparable weather. No wind. Calm and very hot. During the afternoon our ship's captain caught a fish, which the English call a shark, of about fifty pounds on a large hook on which at least a quarter pound of pork had been fastened. It tasted fairly good.

Friday, the 19th of July - Wind and sea raged quite wildly and almost amounted to a complete storm. The water, during the morning, was so rough that it appeared the ship sailed between the most lofty cliffs, into which it was momentarily expected to crash. Our noon meal, usual during a storm, was eaten with all sorts of difficulties. The storm abated at eight o'clock in the evening. At that time we had a splendid theater before us. Everywhere the marvels of nature were to be seen. On one side the beautiful stormy sky could be seen with its stars and the moon in the first quarter. On the other side an artistic cloud-lined horizon was seen which was lighted by the most exceptional lightning flashes. Finally, all around were stormy waves, which gradually calmed.

Saturday, the 20th of July - Very good and warm weather. Wind and sea calm. Little headway.

Sunday, the 21st of July - Quite exceptionally good weather but also quite unbearably hot. The wind favorable. We sailed four or five miles per hour. This evening was exceptionally pleasant and until eleven o'clock we remained on deck. [Code that I can not decipher.]

Monday, the 22nd of July - The heat was very great, little wind and almost calm. The evening pleasant.

Tuesday, the 23rd of July - Beautiful weather. Very hot. The wind good but weak. At nine o'clock in the evening an American privateer was seen. The admiral informed all of the ships about that news and ordered that they stay as close

Bardeleben Diary

together as possible. The frigate immediately began cruising about and sailed far ahead.

Wednesday, the 24th of July - During the previous night a severe storm. It began at two o'clock and lasted until three-thirty in the morning. After the storm it rained very heavily until nine o'clock in the morning. The storm moved along the horizon all day. It was so hot that it was almost impossible to go on deck. This morning the captain caught a five or six foot dolphin. It had many small fish nearby, some of which were of a special species, that is flying fish, which had the form of ordinary fish but with wings which were like a fan and attached to its body and lay close on each side. Others were small and quite narrow. Their mouth looked like a woodcock's bill. We also saw a type of fish yesterday evening, one of which flew onto the ship and hit a soldier in the back of the head.

Thursday, the 25th of July - An exceptional heat. We made little headway. There was lightning during the evening.

Friday, the 26th of July - Early in the morning there was thunder and rain. At nine o'clock in the morning we again had good weather. It was terribly hot all day. We sailed two or two and one-half miles per hour.

Saturday, the 27th of July - Good weather all day. The heat unbearable. No wind and calm. At noon our ship's captain went to another ship. While he was gone, the mate and several sailors became very drunk. One of the sailors was so drunk that he jumped into the ocean several times and each time was again pulled out with the help of a rope.

Sunday, the 28th of July - Terribly hot. The wind fairly good, but we were not allowed to sail on until seven o'clock in the evening. This fate, not being allowed to sail with the favorable wind, we have had for some weeks already. The reason can not be understood. First, we think the rebels occupy every place and have closed off all entrances to the harbors. Then we think that the commander of our fleet has certain information and therefore delays our journey. Therefore everyone is angry and disgusted, but still baffled. [Code that I can not decipher.]

At two o'clock in the afternoon the ship's captain and I went to the ship *Unanimity*, on which the dispute arose between Count von der Lippe and Lieutenant Kleinschmidt. Lieutenant [Christoph] Bode, Lieutenant [Justus Heinrich] Ernst, and Ensign [Johann Anton] Germer, all of the Leib Regiment, were on board that ship. Those officers told me that the cause of the dispute was only over treatment of a dog which Lieutenant Kleinschmidt owned. As he went about the deck, he misstepped and this caused the dog to begin to howl. The Count heard this in his cabin and immediately ran out on deck and asked what had happened to the dog and who had mistreated it. Lieutenant Kleinschmidt explained with diffidence that he had accidently bumped the dog and nothing else had occurred. However, the Count immediately went to his cabin, secretly took out his pistols, and so abused Kleinschmidt that Kleinschmidt had no choice but to shoot him. The officers in the cabin however, knew nothing of all that until the Count entered and told them he was wounded. He lived another 27 hours, and prior to dying wrote for the officers that no one else was responsible and especially that the other officers in the cabin knew nothing of the affair. The interrogation of the Count had been considered very open and serious, and because until the last hour of his death, he was still rational, he was questioned about the whole incident by the chief auditor Motz.

Monday, the 29th of July - Good weather and not nearly so hot. The wind fair. We sailed well. During the evening there was frequent lightning.

Tuesday, the 30th of July - From three o'clock this morning until six o'clock this evening the wind and sea were extremely restless and equally as strong as on 19 July. It also rained very hard and continuously. There was also thunder and lightning at times. At eight o'clock in the evening everything was peaceful and suddenly almost calm. We ate our noon meal hurriedly. It consisted of a serving of cooked pudding without the least butter or other fat, but tasted good. There was not a bit left over. If only it had been larger.

Wednesday, the 31st of July - The past night was very restless. The weather today rather good. We made some headway, but instead of forward, backward. We were in the Gulf Stream from Florida. Today we had to begin drinking water. Our beer had turned sour from the constant heat. Also, our own provisions ran out at the same time. Therefore, from today on, a more Spartan life began and we had to make do with the ordinary ship's rations and, of necessity, the half-stinking water.

Thursday, the 1st of August - Excellent weather but no wind and calm. At two o'clock in the afternoon Captain and Lieutenant Donop, Lieutenant Colonel Heymell, Mr. Sahe, with Ensign von Geyso of the von Knyphausen Regiment and four other ships' captains came aboard our ship. One of these ships' captains was most welcome. He delivered 48 bottles of porter beer at one groschen, also twelve pounds of sugar at fourteen groschen a pound. Once again we lived well. It was no longer necessary to drink water.

Friday, the 2nd of August - Good weather this morning. At four o'clock in the afternoon the seas were running very high and very rough. The same weather as on 30 July. This continued with the heaviest rain gusts until seven o'clock in the evening. Thereafter the wind and weather were fair. Extremely hot late in the evening with frequent lightning. We made good headway.

Saturday, the 3rd of August - Good weather. Very hot. No wind and calm. During the evening the wind was a bit stronger and generally favorable. Our ship's captain caught a shark today, eleven German feet long,[14] and weighing nearly 300

****

14. A German foot is equivalent to an English foot.

Bardeleben Diary

pounds, but it was inedible. Therefore it was cut up and thrown overboard. This species of fish varies and only one type is edible. The flesh of the others is too tough.

Sunday, the 4th of August - Very good weather and not too warm. We sailed well. During the afternoon two ship's captains came aboard our ship.

Monday, the 5th of August -The weather like yesterday's. The wind good and we sailed well. Two ship's captains came aboard our ship.

Tuesday, the 6th of August - Yesterday's weather. We sailed well in the morning. During the afternoon however, little wind and calm. This afternoon a frigate signaled, with a cannon shot and with a pennant on the middle mast, that it could see land. Nothing could be seen from our ship, however. Shortly thereafter, however, everyone was wildly excited. Four ship's captains, who visited our captain today, based on their charts, considered this news to be possible, and although none of us could see anything, each of us now had to see every cloud as a strip of land. This evening we had several visitors. The ships' captains had drunk too much punch in their celebrating. They gathered in the cabin, thereby greatly disturbing our rest. At eleven o'clock in the evening two of the gentlemen departed. However, the others continued drinking just as hard, into the night. We had gone to bed but had to get up again soon thereafter. Suddenly there was a general uproar. Our mate and the carpenter had drunk too much, had a dispute, and began fighting so that the blood covered their hands. We were able to calm them down and fortunately were able to quiet down all those stupid individuals. The two ships' captains, however, remained on our ship overnight. This day has been one of the most unpleasant of our entire voyage.

Wednesday, the 7th of August - Warm weather. Calm in the morning. Some wind in the afternoon. We sailed well, but saw no land.

Bardeleben Diary

Thursday, the 8th of August - Yesterday's weather. Calm all day. Frequent lightning during the evening. Still no land.

Friday, the 9th of August - The same weather. Calm all day. During the evening a heavy fog moved in.

Saturday, the 10th of August - Wind and weather exceptionally fine. At mid-morning we definitely saw land.

Sunday, the 11th of August - Excellent weather. At five o'clock we finally saw the coast of York Island. It is far more splendid than that of England. Here the seacoasts are only forests and there, in England, bare white cliffs. There was the greatest joy throughout the fleet. How fortunate for us to have reached our destination (Gluck au)! - [a miner's greeting meaning good luck or God's speed] because there is already a shortage of almost all foodstuffs. The King's rations were spoiled, the water quite stinking, and also scarce. A large part of the troops have scurvy and other illnesses. For my part, praise God, I am still healthy and have remained free of all accidents.

Monday, the 12th of August - At seven o'clock this morning we were already quite close to the land. At nine o'clock in the morning a fleet of 214 ships joined ours. It was General [Werner] von Mirbach with his own regiment, that of [Johann Gottlieb] von [sic] Rall,[15] and one company of the von Knyphausen Regiment, all those which due to the shortage of shipping had remained behind at Bremerlehe.[16] At eleven o'clock noon we were near Sandy Hook where most of the ships dropped anchor. Our ship sailed farther up the Hudson River. The entrance to this harbor is very pleasant. We sailed past shores lined with hills and fir trees, to the entrance to New York, where we anchored at five o'clock in the evening in a sea nearly

****

15. The author refers to Colonel Rall as von Rall in every mention of the name although the von is incorrect.

16. This was the 2nd Section of the 1st Division which had sailed from Germany on 9 June 1776.

surrounded by land. Toward noon, we had an excellent view, a short distance from the open sea.

Tuesday, the 13th of August - At eleven o'clock noon the admiral gave a signal that the ships should approach as near as possible to Staten Island. We anchored again at one o'clock. From this point we could see the English who were in camp on Staten Island. We also learned here that the rebels occupied everywhere else. Only this small island was free. The ship *Surprise*, with Captain Venator and which we had thought lost, had lain here at anchor already for eight days. Good weather. Terribly hot.

Wednesday, the 14th of August - Our Grenadiers, Jaegers, and some English regiments landed at eleven o'clock noon. We also received orders to be ready to land tomorrow. During the afternoon Captain Venator and Lieutenant Nagel, Sr., visited us. They told us that because of the fog they could not find us again, and their ship's captain had not been sorry to leave the fleet.

Bardeleben Diary
Staten Island

Some inhabitants from Long Island fled here to place themselves under the protection of the English.

Thursday, the 15th of August - We landed at nine o'clock in the morning. The entire army of about 25,000 men was here on Staten Island. Our camp site was excellent. The smell of cedar, sassafras, and other local woods made it very pleasant. There was a scarcity of fresh food. Every effort was made to obtain it but in part because of the English, and before them the rebels, had used it, even on land, we had only ship's rations to eat. Almost no vegetables were to be seen. Now and then potatoes were available. These, and occasionally wheat and Indian or Turkish corn, appear to be the only common fruit. In the woods lemons or wild lemons, walnuts, acorns, chestnuts, and such are found and more, very often a great many poisonous plants. Good weather.

Friday, the 16th of August - Last night was the first in camp. I slept exceptionally well. However, upon awakening it did not clearly register that I was on solid ground, and further, suddenly everywhere, everything, looked warlike to me. I looked around, even walked around, and did this time and again, but still could not get adjusted to the idea. I could not believe that I was in America. Very hot. I bathed.

Saturday, the 17th of August - Nothing new. I went hunting but saw nothing but some ducks, a few of which I shot. Most of our officers must cut the rank insignia from their uniforms, supposedly because the rebel so-called riflemen had their greatest interest in officers, and so that these will not be distinguishable from the privates, gold and silver insignia will not be worn, and now in many regiments all uniforms are similar. Our regiment continued without change. Terribly hot.

Sunday, the 18th of August - Rain during the entire past night which continued until twelve o'clock noon. Although the rain beat through my tent, I slept well. At five o'clock in the morning there was a heavy cannonade between some frigates and the rebels in the batteries of New York City. Those frigates had taken a position on the North River in order to bombard the city. Today, however, they had to return to the fleet. In the process of passing the forts lying at the point of the city, they drew a heavy fire against themselves. One ship lost the middle mast. The firing continued intermittently until one o'clock in the morning.

Monday, the 19th of August - At seven o'clock in the morning the Prince Charles, Leib, Truembach, and Ditfurth Regiments, which were near us, had to change their camp and take the post which the English, who had been ordered to board ship, had occupied. Quite good weather.

Tuesday, the 20th of August - Our Grenadiers and the English Light Infantry were ordered to be ready to march. Warm weather.

Wednesday, the 21st of August - From seven o'clock yesterday evening until one o'clock at night we had the most terrible weather. No one could remember ever having had such a storm. Lightning, thunder claps, storms, and driving rain, all in extremes. My tent, surrounded by a constant fire, seemed to tremble with the ground at every thunder peal. At ten o'clock in the evening three English brigades and our Grenadiers and Jaegers embarked on some transport ships and lay at anchor at a certain distance from Long Island. Very hot.

Thursday, the 22nd of August - At six o'clock in the morning the embarked brigades, a few hundred cavalry, as well as the English Light Infantry, Grenadiers, and Scots were landed on Long Island from small boats. The warships had lain for some time as close to the shore as possible in order to provide support against any resistance. Although the rebels had a strength of more than 5,000 men and if needed could have been reinforced quickly from New York, they allowed our troops to land unopposed and made not the least resistance. Our corps immediately advanced and occupied the level fields and the nearby lying city of Flatbush, without being bothered by the rebels. They bivouacked at night. A short distance from their front the rebels were posted on a height and in the woods. Very hot. I bathed.

Friday, the 23rd of August - I had duty at the outposts. Now the troops receive fresh meat and a pickled sauerkraut, and porter beer was delivered. Very hot weather.

Saturday, the 24th of August - The Stirn and Mirbach Brigades had to change camp, extend [their fronts], and one regiment had to occupy the space for two regiments. Good weather.

Sunday, the 25th of August - [Marginal Note - Colonel von Lossberg remained behind on Staten Island with the Ditfurth, Prince Charles, and Truembach Regiments, and 500 English under Colonel [William] Dalrymple.] The two brigades mentioned above, namely the Hereditary Prince, von Donop, and von Mirbach, von Knyphausen, von Lossberg, and von [sic] Rall Regiments were transferred across to Long Island. We joined the others and camped in the region of Flatbush. The Grenadiers were on our right. Their pickets were continuously alerted. Two deserters brought the report that they had received a reinforcement of 3,000 men from New York and planned to attack us in our camp. All our posts were doubled and the Grenadiers were ordered to remain dressed all night. Very hot.

Monday, the 26th of August - [Marginal Note - As the enemy had a detachment in the woods in our front, they attacked single outposts now and then, from that place. To prevent this, Colonel [Heinrich Anton von] Heringen ordered the pickets of Stirn and Mirbach Brigades, which amounted to 250 men, to occupy a mill lying on the water to our left.] The two brigades, Stirn and Mirbach, changed camp and marched one mile farther inland. On this march signs of the enemy's mood were found everywhere. During their flight from our initial landing on this island they left behind burned out houses, grain standing in the fields, some of it in ashes, and the road was lined with dead

Bardeleben Diary

cattle. Now and again old people, with sad glances, looked back at their homes, which the flames had destroyed and which appeared previously to have been a paradise standing in blooming abundance. Our regiment was camped amidst orchards of apple and pear trees; our tents were all covered over and shaded by the trees. Here, too, the picture of destruction was to be seen on all sides. Almost everywhere there were chests of drawers, chairs, mirrors with gold-gilded frames, porcelain, and all sorts of items of the best and most expensive manufacture. It was sad to see how all this and also our things, misused and destroyed, were laying about. At seven o'clock in the evening the Scots and English marched off and took positions far beyond our right wind, in order to try to attack the enemy's rear. Quite good weather.

Tuesday, the 27th of August - Early, before daybreak, a heavy firing was heard beyond our right wing. It was soon learned that the English and Scots who had marched yesterday evening had fallen on the enemy flank and attacked. (The commanding general-in-chief had not informed Lieutenant [General] von Heister of this plan.) [Marginal Note - General Howe gave the English the following order yesterday. The army will break camp this evening, 26 August. The advance guard of the column: Lieutenant General [Henry] Clinton with three battalions of Light Infantry, four battalions of Grenadiers, the 33rd and 71st Regiments; Lieutenant General [Charles, Earl] Cornwallis has Major Generals [Hugh, Lord] Percy, [Alexander] Leslie, and [William] Erskine under his command, plus six 6-pound cannons and four 3-pound cannons and two howitzers. The Brigade of Guards on the front with General Percy will have two 6-pound cannons and two howitzers, and be the advance guard. The second brigade will have two 6-pound cannons. The third brigade will have two 12-pound cannons and the 49th Regiment, four 12-pound cannons. The last mentioned will be the rear guard. The fourth, fifth, and sixth brigades will have six 6-pound cannons, two 3-pound cannons, and two howitzers

Bardeleben Diary

with them and will receive special marching orders.] At seven o'clock in the morning we broke camp also. Our Grenadiers closed to the English on our right and formed the middle [of the line]. The other Hessian regiments occupied all the heights and valleys around the woods. Shortly after taking their positions, the English had already overrun the enemy flank and the enemy retreated to the heights in the center, where our Grenadiers had planned to take post. However, even here it was necessary for the enemy to withdraw farther without being able to make any resistance. Because of the landscape and the terrible hills, they could not be attacked *en masse*, but only by groups. All the regiments at once sent strong patrols, as strong as possible, in general, to attack the enemy. Only then did a general engagement begin. The enemy, who was surrounded on all sides by small arms fire, suddenly fell into the greatest confusion, scattered, and thereafter soon fell into our hands, first to this patrol and then to the next, completely cut up, without having offered any great resistance. I was sent with some volunteers into a woods laying in front of us to seek out that which could be found.

[Code that I can not decipher.]

I saw nothing. One of our soldiers found a silver mounted knife. Another patrol from our regiment brought in many prisoners, however.

[Code - Many high ranking individuals at this time shed their ideas of being heroes. The prisoners who knelt and sought to surrender were beaten.] This skirmish lasted four or five hours. According to all estimates, the rebels suffered 1,200 dead and wounded and 1,097 prisoners, including 3 generals, 3 colonels, 4 lieutenant colonels, 3 majors, 18 captains, 43 lieutenants, 11 ensigns, 1 adjutant, 1 surgeon, and 1 volunteer; 20 cannons, almost all 24 and 32-pounders. The loss for the English was 1 lieutenant colonel, 3 captains, 1 lieutenants, 3 sergeants and 53 privates killed; 1 lieutenant colonel, 3 captains, 8 lieutenants, 11 sergeants, 3 drummers, and 250 privates

Bardeleben Diary

wounded; 1 lieutenant, 1 sergeant, and 20 privates missing. The Hessians suffered 2 privates killed and 25 privates wounded. All the other rebels fled, part into the defenses which they had at Brooklyn Ferry, directly opposite New York, and part hid in the woods. The rebels were pursued on this day and attacked in their defenses with great success and their entire strength of 10,000 men, which had occupied this island, would have been ours if the commander-in-chief had not called a halt. All the regiments had to remain in their camps, under arms, this entire night, because the woods had not been cleared [of rebels]. The clothing of the enemy is bad. A few wear black, white, or violet linen, short blouses with fringes, and of a Spanish style. They also have a linen sack in which they carry their rations, and a powder horn. Others, on the other hand, have nothing but a wretched farmer's costume and a weapon. Most of their officers are no better dressed and until recently were only ordinary manual laborers. Lieutenant General von Heister, who remained with our regiment during this affair, had all the prisoners captured by the Hessians brought to him and then held them under a detachment behind our regiment. A number of wounded were treated and others were gradually sent from here to where they could be more safely guarded. His Excellence engaged in conversation with several rebel officers and gave them wine with which to drink the health of the King of England. One of these officers, however, who was a well-situated schoolmaster, refused to accept the glass because he did not want to drink the King's health. He was told and threatened with being shot dead on the spot if he continued to act like a rebel here. Nevertheless, all the threats were to no avail. He answered in each instance, that he was a school teacher and because he felt it a duty of his position and had tried with all his efforts to instruct his students never to declare themselves for the King, he would gladly sacrifice his life and lose everything before he would change his sentiment.

[Code that I can not decipher.]

Bardeleben Diary

Wednesday, the 28th of August - At six o'clock in the morning the Stirn and Mirbach Brigades moved back to their previous camp. Our Grenadiers and some English remained in advance positions in order to immediately set up camp. At one o'clock in the afternoon we also followed and set up camp near them on a height beyond Bedford. Our camps were directly opposite the enemy and only a small arm of the sea separated us. From two o'clock in the afternoon until seven o'clock in the evening, even as we moved into camp, it rained without letup and very heavily. Our tents were so wet that they were barely able to keep out the water.

In such a rain I was sent out with a detachment of thirty men to help cover our regiment (or so I was told, at least). It appears to be the general's intention in this war to be very deliberate in his efforts. Two English soldiers came with the order for our colonel that the pickets were to hurry with the two soldiers to the support of an English detachment which had been pinned down under fire for some time. I marched with my troops to the desired location. Instead, however, of covering the regiment, I was sent about two miles away from it. I arrived at my designated position and, according to my orders, reported to an English major under whose command several pickets served. This major ordered me, as one of his pickets, with the definite instruction to take my post immediately. Because I did not know where I was, had no knowledge of where the rebels were, nor what forces were to my left or rear, I asked for the information first. However, the major gave me this answer, I could place the posts at my discretion. The rebels had their many posts about 200 yards away, and he did not know what lay to left of in our rear.

First I sought to insure that my troops and I were secure and set posts before, to the left, and behind us. Then I sent out patrols. By so doing I learned that our rear was secure, but far to the left we had no one. If the rebels had only a little courage and determination all of our pickets could have been captured.

Bardeleben Diary

Because I did not have enough men to occupy this pass, I detached a non-commissioned officer with a few soldiers to go there and also sent out frequent patrols.

Thursday, the 29th of August - The night was quiet and no rebels were seen. Some of my troops fired, but it was too dark to be able to recognize anyone. In the morning, before daybreak, my command was reinforced by six jaegers and one officer and twenty men moved up on my left. As soon as it was light the rebels began moving about a great deal and began working diligently on their defenses. Many also risked sneaking up on us. The Jaegers fired at them, wounding several. Their audacity disappeared and they sought revenge. They had barely regained their redoubt when they opened fire with cannons and cannonaded us. Their aim was excellent. As soon as two or three men were seen, a cannonball was on its way and often hit near the sentries. At seven o'clock in the morning they ceased this activity and everything was quiet. I was relieved at seven o'clock in the evening by Captain Venator with two officers and 100 men, who were then fully capable of occupying my posts. Marching back to camp I lost the way and had to go a long way before I found the camp. I had almost feared falling into the rebels' hands, as it was impossible to see your hand before your face. I marched from one [camp] to the next until I finally entered a Hessian camp, where I received the necessary directions. All day long rebels had been brought in who had hidden in the woods on the 27th and sought thus to escaped to return to their troops.

Friday, the 30th of August - In the morning no enemies were to be seen. They had evacuated all their defenses and taken flight during the past night. Lieutenant Colonel [Ernst Rudolph] von Schieck, who commanded all the pickets and detachments, discovered their flight at daybreak. He immediately advanced, sent a captain with ninety grenadiers into the enemy lines, and 24 of these men then occupied their largest position. General [James] Grant, who commanded the left wing, had the brigade of Colonel von Donop follow at once. At three o'clock in the afternoon the von Lossberg and von Donop Regiments occupied the enemy defenses opposite New York, as well as those houses lying along the shore. The enemy had in part crossed to New York at Brooklyn Ferry and in part gone to Red Hook, a small, nearby island.

The rebel defenses of the so-called Brooklyn Line were of the type that determined troops could have held against a far stronger enemy than we were. They had star fortifications on the wings. The line itself also had the same. The right wing was also protected by a marsh and woods, and was also strengthened by small outworks and an abatis. Also on this wing there was a large battery on Red Hook Island, to cover the channel from New York and the woods. The left wing was protected by a strong abatis. The front had double palisades the entire length of the trenches, half trenches, and all surrounded by an abatis. Behind these defenses, on all the hills, were redoubts, some well-started, some finished, including one small redoubt with a casement for 300 men provided with rations, and the so-called Sterling Redoubt, which was occupied by five companies, both lying opposite New York and being the most significant. At every position we found a great amount of provisions and ammunition, and many cannons, although most were spiked. Our regiment occupied three positions lying along the shore. In one of these, where I was, there were 250 and three staff officers. Toward five o'clock in the evening the English Artillery joined us with four 24-pound cannons, in order to fire upon a detachment of about 200 rebels who were directly ahead of us on a small island called Governor's Island, and who were being transferred to New York in small boats. Firing against these had barely commenced when the order arrived to cease fire. As it did not cease immediately, two boats occupied by about twenty men were sunk by the English.

Saturday, the 31st of August - At six o'clock in the evening the von Knyphausen Regiment relieved us. We returned

Bardeleben Diary

to our camp. Governor's Island was occupied this evening by a captain, two officers, and 100 men, who were taken there in sloops. Otherwise everything was peaceful. Good weather.

Sunday, the 1st of September - The whole army changed camp and moved along the edge of the water to Brooklyn opposite New York; the English on the right, the Scots on the left, and the Hessians in the middle. Good weather.

Monday, the 2nd of September - Four 18-pound cannons and six 32-pound cannons were found on Governor's Island. I took a walk in the afternoon. The local region is splendid and diverse. The whole island appears to be an Elysium. In all the fields the finest fruit is to be found. The peach and apple trees are especially numerous. The local villages and rural houses present a pleasant and changing scenery. From one village to the next, from one rural home to the next, the roads are very good and all are lined with apple trees. The houses, in part, are made only of wood and the furnishings in them are excellent. Comfort, beauty, and cleanliness are readily apparent. Above all, the exteriors of the houses show an Italian influence which suits the houses very nicely. Good weather.

Tuesday, the 3rd of September - Nothing new. Good weather.

Wednesday, the 4th through the 9th of September - Everything very peaceful. Beautiful weather.

Tuesday, the 10th of September -The enemy daily made more defenses on the shore on his side. Therefore great preparations were made on our side, also, not however, with the intent of using the same, but only as a plan, because the enemy thought we would land near the city. In three or four places batteries were set up opposite the enemy's. At five o'clock in the evening, therefore, I was ordered to take 120 men and remove boards, beams, and everything of use from the various and formerly enemy defenses [on Long Island]. This was completed at ten o'clock. These items were then loaded in wagons and taken away. Shortly before daybreak we arrived at the shore at

Bardeleben Diary

Brooklyn Ferry, where our batteries were being set up. It rained all night and was dark.

Wednesday, the 11th of September - At six o'clock in the morning I was relieved. In order to prevent being harassed by the enemy, the shore had been lined with heavy branches and the laborers were able to work peacefully (on the batteries) without being seen. By evening the batteries were nearly all finished. They were immediately supplied with cannons. In the two batteries near the Remsen's Mill, not far from the ferry, four 12-pound cannons and four howitzers were placed; in those near Hellgate, a battery with two 24-pound cannons, four 12-pound cannons, and two howitzers. This mask alerted the rebels and after they discovered our works, they immediately opened fire. Good weather.

Thursday, the 12th of September -The enemy was seen to be strengthening his defenses and seemed not to be suspicious but took all precautionary measures to make our landing difficult. Both sides kept up a constant cannonade. The enemy also tried to approach our shore in small boats at night, but because the shore was protected by pickets, the enemy could never accomplish their mission, although this resulted in a heavy small arms fire. At six o'clock in the evening I went on a command to the ferry to occupy the water [front]. Good weather.

Friday, the 13th of September - I was relieved at six o'clock in the evening by the lieutenant. Nothing happened during my watch and nothing is expected. During the night, at one of my defense posts, some suspicious people apparently had planned to cross to the rebels. The firing from the batteries continued, toward evening, very heavy. Five frigates went past New York. The enemy fired continuously at those ships from their batteries on York [Manhattan Island], but the ships [passed] fortunately. At present our side is able to fire upon the enemy defenses very heavily. At noon the army received orders at the first hint of daybreak to be ready to move out with two

Bardeleben Diary

days' provisions. However, counter orders arrived during the evening to remain in camp. Good weather.

Saturday, the 14th of September - The order of yesterday to be ready to march was repeated. At eight o'clock in the evening we were notified to break camp tomorrow at daybreak. Good weather.

Sunday, the 15th of September - [Marginal Note - Lieutenant General von Heister, with six English regiments and the von Mirbach Brigade, remained in camp on Long Island. - the von Mirbach Brigade - von Lossberg, von Knyphausen, and von [sic] Rall Regiments.] At three o'clock in the morning we broke camp and marched along the South River to the place where the troops were to be embarked. The baggage was left behind. At nine o'clock in the morning we arrived at our designated place and found the small boats, which came from the warships that had arrived during the night, waiting. At ten o'clock in the morning the English Light Infantry, the Scots, our Grenadiers and Jaegers, and a part of the English with a little artillery were embarked. Each small boat could carry sixty or seventy men. Five warships, which were in the East River to protect the crossing, took these boats between them and sailed briefly on the water. The rebels, who had only a few batteries and guns in their lines on the shore, seemed confused by these various maneuvers by the ships and could not determine where we would land. Soon the frigates drew together, formed a line as near as possible to the shore, and fired a terrible cannonade against the enemy batteries and guns. The enemy evacuated his lines under this cannonade and pulled back into the woods. Our troops landed without the least resistance being made. They immediately formed with the English on the right, the Grenadiers on the left, and marched off against the enemy who had quickly sought shelter a few hundred yards ahead of them in a woods. Our forces attacked by companies. The Block Grenadier Battalion, which constituted the left wing, encountered a rebel regiment of 500 men, which indicated it wished to surrender.

Bardeleben Diary

However, when the battalion approached, the regiment fled, firing a general volley backward from weapons lying over their shoulders. This killed two men and wounded thirteen. A colonel, two captains, a brigade major, five lieutenants, and 47 privates, of the 500 rebels, were captured. At four o'clock in the afternoon the rest of the English and General Stirn's Brigade were transferred across the river. (The von Mirbach Brigade remained on Long Island.) Stirn's Brigade followed the others, without, however, making contact with the enemy. After a march of three to four English miles, the troops halted at a good position. The garrison at New York abandoned the city as soon as they heard of our landing, marching alongside the North River and then occupied the forts in that area.

Monday, the 16th of September - Our situation during the past night was not pleasant. It was so terribly cold all night that despite our many and large fires, there was no protection from the cold. We lay in bushes and the area seemed to have more rocks than dirt. The rural homes in this region suffered some, even much, damage. All their livestock was seized; also all other useful items were not left lying about. And never before have so many geese, chickens, ducks, cattle, and pigs been slaughtered, as were killed during the night from yesterday evening to this morning. Very early this morning a strong enemy troop moved into position ahead of the English outposts and immediately attacked the Light Infantry. (The Light Infantry as well as our Grenadiers and Jaegers were in front of us.) The troop drove the English into their outer defenses. When the enemy discovered the weakness of the English, his forces were reinforced by a new corps of 2,000 or 3,000 men which attacked these three regiments. The English reserve, the Linsing Grenadier Battalion and the Jaegers, with two field pieces, hurried forward to assist while the Minnigerode and Block Grenadier Battalions occupied the defile along both sides of the road to New York, to cover the rear. As a result the enemy was driven back into his outer defenses with heavy losses. The Scots and Light Infantry suffered seventy dead and 150 wounded during this affair. Our Jaegers had one officer, Lieutenant [Johannes] Heinrich, and seven men wounded. Good weather.

Tuesday, the 17th of September - [Marginal Note - General [James] Robertson was named commandant of New York and entered the city with the 54th and a part of the 5th Regiments.] Our brigade, as well as the rest of the army, spent the night in bivouac and it was very cold again. At eight o'clock in the morning some English and grenadiers marched about two and one-half miles back from their posts and sat up camp near Bloomingdale. Our brigade followed at two o'clock in the afternoon. We marched forward three or four English miles and, possibly because someone had forgotten to assign us a campsite, we had to remain on a tree-lined country road. I felt the sharp coldness of the night. Because of the terrible heat of the day, I had worn only a light uniform. Good weather.

Wednesday, the 18th of September - At eight o'clock in the morning we marched into camp close to the place where we had been two nights before. We had received our tents a short time previously. We were located not far behind the English and Grenadiers, on a small hill close to the banks of the North River. The enemy was once again in his defenses, part on this side, part on the other side of Kingsbridge. As soon as we settled in camp, I was sent with several wagons to get provisions and returned at two o'clock in the afternoon. Very hot.

Thursday, the 19th of September - Nothing new. All quiet. Good weather.

Friday, the 20th of September - I went on picket duty. Nothing new. Good weather.

Saturday, the 21st of September - During the past night the rebels set fire to a number of places in New York. At midnight the flames broke out everywhere in the northern part of the city. A strong wind helped their plan. More than 500 houses, including the best in the city, and the English and Lutheran churches were victims of the flames. Those inhabitants, who could save almost nothing from this disaster and who were taken by surprise during their sleep by this midnight fire, were fortunate to save their lives. The English Grenadier Brigade, which was in camp just outside the city, hurried there along with the sailors and by nine o'clock in the morning had prevented the entire city from being laid in ashes. Everything was in confusion and the garrison had difficulty restoring order. Several persons were arrested, who were running about with incendiary materials with which to set additional fires. The evil intentions of this nation can not be described. One, disturbed at his intended activity and who had to flee, called back during his flight that if he could not carry out his intent, he would still find opportunity later to set fire in the city. Another, who planned to set his own house on fire, but who was prevented from doing so by his wife who hugged him and tearfully asked him not to do so, was so cruel that when his wife would not let go of him, he nearly cut her hand off with his knife. The soldiers, who came to her rescue, grabbed this malcontent and hanged him without ceremony on his own house. Several other suspicious persons were now and again thrown into the flames.

The city is open for the most part. Only on the nearby Governor's Island is there a strong fort, which has been established since the city was captured. The rebels had lined all the shores with cannons and cannons were set up to within two and one-half miles of the city. Primarily the island is heavily fortified everywhere and almost everywhere some means of defense has been set up. Otherwise this island does not have the pleasant situation of Long Island.

Sunday, the 22nd of September - At eight o'clock this morning our brigade marched closer to New York along the North River. The tents were left behind. We joined some English regiments which were to be embarked with us. [Marginal Note - In order to make a landing at Paulus Hook].

Bardeleben Diary

However, countermanding orders arrived and at eleven o'clock noon we marched back into our camp. Warm weather.

Monday, the 23rd of September - I rode to New York, The fire still burned in several places near the North River. [Even] the worst houses were occupied and there was almost nothing unoccupied. The shortage of money is noticeable everywhere and only paper money was in use. It already has no value, except that which has the royal seal has the same value as gold and silver. Good weather.

Tuesday, the 24th of September - An English regiment landed on Paulus Hook under the cover of a warship. This peninsula had to be occupied according to the plan so that the enemy could not fire on the city. Until today the rebels still had one which fired intermittently on the city. but upon the approach of the warship, it had been withdrawn. Good weather. At ten o'clock in the morning our brigade was mustered.

Wednesday, the 25th of September - The Grenadier Battalion was mustered, also, by an English commissary. Dysentery is rampant in the Hessian corps and a great many lay dangerously ill from its effects. In our regiment I was almost the only one free of the disease. Good weather.

Thursday, the 26th of September - Lieutenant General Howe began raising provincial regiments. General [Oliver] DeLancey was in charge of the recruiting and made Hamster on Long Island the assembly point. Although that island is under control of the King's weapons, there are still many secret traitors thereon. They seek only a slight advantage before showing their rebel inclinations. One of the officers of the mentioned [provincial] corps is a proof of this. He was secretly shot by a resident when on his way from Bedford to Flatbush. Today Colonel Heringen of the Lossberg Regiment was buried. He died of dysentery from which we have lost many and still a large number of men lie dangerously ill. Good weather.

Bardeleben Diary

Friday, the 27th of September - I went on guard in the city. The posts were along the shore of the North River. Good weather.

Saturday, the 28th of September - Nothing new. Good weather.

Sunday, the 29th of September - Nothing new. Good weather. Two frigates sailed up the North River and lay to at two different places to help cover the camp.

Monday, the 30th of September - I went on patrol. Nothing new. Good weather.

Bardeleben Diary

Tuesday, the 1st of October - At nine o'clock in the morning our brigade changed camp and moved ahead of our Grenadiers in order to somewhat lighten their strenuous service as well as to encourage them so that they could more quickly move out. We set up our tents close to the North River and our regiment was on the left wing. We occupied the defenses here which in part had been constructed by us and the English and made a chain not far from the enemy lines. A thick woods about a mile wide divided our camp. The English outposts are on the right wing close to the Harlem River, hardly a rifle shot away from the rebels. Our main command post was quite near our camp, in a gentleman's house from which the inhabitants had fled, but in which many items remained. Among other items, much wine, silverware, and chests of drawers. One which we found was of great value and estimated to have a value in our money of more than 200 dollars. Some jaegers also occupied this house, who because our brigade furnished the commands, were required to go on patrol, but had no other duties.

Wednesday, the 2nd of October - I went on a command at the mentioned house with Captain [Ludwig] Winckelmann of the Hereditary Prince Regiment. The senior officer with thirty men was in the lead and the captain was detached fifty yards farther to the north, and beyond that officer, another officer with twelve men manned the outposts. All of these detachments went to their posts at four o'clock in the morning.

Thursday, the 3rd of October - During the patrol nothing occurred. The night was cold and at present the nights are really very cold. Fourteen ships carrying an English regiment of light dragoons arrived today and were quartered in New York.

Friday, the 4th of October - Nothing new. Good weather. I rode into New York.

Saturday, the 5th of October - Nothing new. Good weather.

Sunday, the 6th of October - Nothing new. Good weather.

Bardeleben Diary

Monday, the 7th of October - I went on duty with the city guard. Good weather. Nothing new.

Tuesday, the 8th of October - Nothing new. Good weather.

Wednesday, the 9th of October - At seven o'clock in the morning three warships sailed up the North River, near our camp, and lay to near Kingsbridge. The ships drew a heavy fire against themselves, even from Fort Lee, which was laid out some time ago on the opposite shore, as well as from Fort Washington and the batteries at that place. An alternating cannonade resulted, so strong that it seemed impossible for ships to pass successfully. Each one, nevertheless, successfully passed between both of those places without damage. Good weather. Rather cold.

Thursday, the 10th of October - At four o'clock in the morning I went on duty in the defenses at the main command post. Good weather.

Friday, the 11th of October - Nothing new during my duty. The night was very cold. At ten o'clock in the evening our Grenadiers and Light Infantry marched to the East River in order to go aboard ship. Lieutenant General Percy now has command over the three brigades here. The brigade commanders are General Stirn, [James] Grant, and Johns [Jones?]. I bathed this afternoon in the North River. At one o'clock last night the Grenadiers and English Light Infantry embarked near Hellgate in eighty sloops. One of those boats, occupied by 25 English artillerymen with three cannons, ran aground there. The cannons and thirteen men were lost and the others saved themselves. At nine o'clock in the morning the troops landed in Connecticut, fifteen English miles from their place of embarkation, and marched inland without meeting any great resistance. During the afternoon Lieutenant General von Heister, with his corps of six English regiments and the von Mirbach Brigade, crossed from Long Island to Connecticut and joined the other troops. Good weather. I bathed. The water is very cold, but felt good.

Sunday, the 13th of October - I went on picket duty. Nothing new. Good weather.

Monday, the 14th of October - Nothing new. Good weather. Twenty provisions ships with 600 recruits arrived. These men had been recruited in Germany for the Scheiter Corps. They were immediately distributed among the English regiments.

Tuesday, the 15th of October - I went on duty at the outposts. Good weather.

Wednesday, the 16th of October - Nothing new. Good weather.

Thursday, the 17th of October -Nothing new. It rained during the afternoon.

Friday, the 18th of October - The English Lieutenant General Howe transferred with his corps to another side of Connecticut, named New Rochelle. Colonel von Lossberg's Regiment, which previously had been on Staten Island, and the Ditfurth, Leib, and Prince Charles Regiments joined the army, leaving only the Truembach Regiment on Staten Island.

Saturday, the 19th of October - On patrol. Good weather.

Sunday, the 20th of October - Nothing new. Good weather. Lieutenant General von Knyphausen arrived with the 2nd Division [of Hesse-Cassel troops], having left Hesse on 11 May 1776.

Monday, the 21st of October - Nothing new. Good weather.

Tuesday, the 22nd of October - I went on duty with thirty men. Good weather. The 2nd Division sailed away in order to join with General Howe's army.

Wednesday, the 23rd of October - Nothing new. Good weather. The 2nd Division landed in the region of New Rochelle on the White Plains.

Bardeleben Diary

Thursday, the 24th of October - Nothing new. Good weather.

Friday, the 25th of October - We received orders to march. Good weather.

Saturday, the 26th of October - During the morning the order came to be ready to depart. Soon thereafter we received a counter-order. Good weather.

Sunday, the 27th of October - At six o'clock in the morning we received orders to be ready to march immediately. At eight o'clock our brigade, less the von Mirbach Regiment which had to remain in camp, and the English moved in front of the enemy lines, not far from Fort Washington. Near, about 2,000 yards, in front of the first abatis, we halted, brought up our cannons, and fired most of the day against the trenches. The enemy appeared to think our attack was a sham and not meant in earnest. They remained quietly in their trenches and laughed at us for firing such a heavy cannonade. Although we were a few thousand yards from them, they fired their rifles so effectively at our outposts, that two guys from the Hereditary Prince Regiment were wounded. In marching through the woods which lay just before our camp, I commanded the leading element and when our regiment halted, I was with a detachment to establish outposts a few hundred yards ahead of the regiment. The von Donop Regiment was on the left wing, and occupied the side from the North River to the command post. The Hereditary Prince Regiment was beside us, and in front of the woods with their command post therein. The English were on the right wing and extended close to the Harlem River, where the enemy lines ended. The rebels fired on all these units sporadically so that no one dared raise his head, and when they saw our posts were to be relieved, ten or fifteen men would fire at the same time. Toward evening everything quieted down. At seven o'clock in the evening I relieved Lieutenant Hausmann and the regiment remained in bivouac at the place where we had initially had our outposts. Good weather.

Bardeleben Diary

Monday, the 28th of October - During the night everything was quiet and no shots were fired by our side during the day. The rebels fired occasionally at our outposts. At seven o'clock in the evening we moved out of our positions and quietly reentered camp, without the enemy being aware of it. [Marginal Note - On this day Lieutenant General von Knyphausen strengthened several forts near Kingsbridge.] On this day His Excellency, Lieutenant General Howe, attacked the enemy at White Plains. As the enemy sent detachments here from there, we had to move forward. The rebels had excellent [positions] at White Plains. They had made their defenses better than usual and maintained their posts with extraordinary tenacity. During the battle the von Lossberg Regiment lost [Scratched out - 3 dead and 47 wounded, Rall 1 dead and 2 wounded; and the English 195 men dead and wounded.] [Marginal Note - English dead - 1 staff officer, 8 subalterns, 137 privates; Hessian dead - 42, wounded 2 officers, Lieutenants [Johann Christoph] Muehlhausen and [Karl von] Rau, and 96 privates.] Good weather.

Tuesday, the 29th of October - Nothing new with us. I went hunting, but shot nothing. Good weather.

Wednesday, the 30th of October - The brigade of General Grant marched to join the army in Connecticut. Four English and three Hessian regiments remained here. The Hereditary Prince Regiment moved to the right. The von Donop and von Mirbach Regiments extended their camps. I went on picket duty.

Thursday, the 31st of October - It rained continuously during the past night and I had not another dry stitch. It rained all day no less heavily and also cold.

Friday, the 1st of November - On reports of another attack pending, the enemy at White Plains withdrew and vacated the heights not far from the city of White Plains. Prior to their retreat some houses in the city were set on fire. Our troops occupied the evacuated heights at once and set up their camp.

Bardeleben Diary

Saturday, the 2nd of November - Lieutenant General von Knyphausen crossed to York Island at Kingsbridge with the Koehler Grenadier Battalion and the Wutginau, Stein, and Wissenbach Regiments. Upon his arrival the enemy pulled back to the defenses before Fort Washington. Those [Hessian] regiments then set up their camp there. In our camp nothing new. The past night ice formed, but not thickly.

Sunday, the 3rd of November - Nothing new. Rather cold. It froze again during the past night. The nights are very cold now and nearly unbearable. Almost all officers and many privates, too, have built huts. They have dug deep holes in the ground and covered the roofs with cases to make surviving the cold easier. I dislike the huts. Our entire camp was constructed of earthen huts and looked quite disorderly.

Monday, the 4th of November - Nothing new. Rather cold. Our troops are sick and continue to die. Lieutenant Colonel Heymell, Major Hinte, and Captain von Donop have lain dangerously ill with dysentery for some weeks.

Tuesday, the 5th of November - There was a heavy cannonade at four o'clock. Two provisions ships went up the North River escorted by a frigate, in order to deliver foodstuffs close to Kingsbridge. The rebels directed fire against the ships from Forts Washington and Lee; and as near as we could see from our camp, the frigate lost a sail.

At five o'clock in the evening I was sent on picket duty with 24 men, and close to the North River, according to plan, so that the enemy would not risk coming from Jersey in boats. The evening was exceptionally pleasant.

Wednesday, the 6th of November - At seven o'clock in the morning I left the picket. The pass was not occupied all day. The night had been cold and it had rained hard. Today was pleasant, however, and nearly as hot as in mid-summer. Lieutenant General Lord Howe evacuated the heights at White Plains and now stands only a few English miles from Kingsbridge, not far from the North River.

Bardeleben Diary

Thursday, the 7th of November - Early in the morning I was sent to New York to get a house in which to store the regimental baggage. Until this time the baggage for all regiments had remained aboard the transport ships and had just now been unloaded. I returned late in the evening. Good weather.

Friday, the 8th of November - At four o'clock in the morning I was sent with a detail of 37 men to occupy the position in front of the main headquarters. Because Lieutenant General von Knyphausen allowed firing against the batteries at Fort Washington, a continuous cannonade was fired throughout the day.

Saturday, the 9th of November - The detail was relieved at seven o'clock in the morning. Nothing new had occurred. The past night had not been cold. Good weather. During the evening I was a member of the reserve picket. [Marginal Note - Lieutenant General von Knyphausen had his outpost between a woods and the road leading to New York. This outpost was attacked today by the rebels. Lieutenant [Johannes] Schwein of the Stein Regiment was killed during the attack and several of his troops were wounded.]

Sunday, the 10th of November - Nothing new. All quiet at our camp. Good weather.

Monday, the 11th of November - Throughout the past night it rained extremely hard, with frightfully strong winds. My tent was soaked and almost nothing therein was dry. Raw weather all day.

Tuesday, the 12th of November - Nothing new at our camp. Good weather.

Wednesday, the 13th of November - Nothing new. Good weather. [Marginal Note - The Commanding General Lord Howe moved from White Plains with the army today and settled on the heights of Kingsbridge.]

Thursday, the 14th of November - Nothing new. Fair weather.

Bardeleben Diary

Friday, the 15th of November - We received the order at five o'clock in the evening to be prepared to attack the enemy lines outside Fort Washington.

Saturday, the 16th of November - At five o'clock in the morning we took up our weapons but only began our march against the enemy line at seven o'clock. After a half-hour march we arrived before it. Several regiments formed at once on the small heights lying opposite the enemy defenses. After all the regimental pieces and several English 12-pound cannons were moved up, from the English on the right and us on the left wing, a prolonged bombardment was fired upon the enemy trenches. During this cannonade the advance guard moved up through a valley lying ahead of us, and the supporting regiments immediately followed. The von Donop Regiment took a position close to the North River and with five accompanying cannons covered the left flank. The rebels, who had no heavy cannons in their line, fired only a few rifle shots against the advance guard from the trenches and then took flight. On the opposite side of Fort Washington, near Kingsbridge, Lieutenant General von Knyphausen attacked with the von [sic] Koehler Grenadier Battalion, the von Lossberg, Rall, and Waldeck Regiments in the first column; the von Wutginau, von Knyphausen, and von Huyn and von Buenau Regiments in the second column. The corps on the other side of Kingsbridge served as a support force as well as to prevent the enemy forces left behind at White Plains from being able to disrupt our forces during the attack. The eight regiments mentioned had to make a more difficult and dangerous attack than we had on this side. Natural and artificial defenses on that entire side were the best, and well-constructed. All the enemy batteries surrounding Fort Washington were on cliffs, whose impossibly steep sides were so rocky and whose abatis of interlocking and nearly insurmountable trees, had to be overcome. However, despite all these hindrances, the two columns, with a most praise-worthy effort, climbed the cliffs and attacked the enemy with such rare energy and such ardor that the enemy had to flee into the main fort in complete confusion, and shortly thereafter to surrender.

By four o'clock in the afternoon all fighting had ceased and terms had been agreed upon. Initially the enemy had requested being allowed to march out free, but this was not allowed. They next asked to be allowed to take out their weapons. With this understanding, and with no further conditions, 3,000 men surrendered.

During the battle the Hessian deaths were 2 captains, 3 subalterns, and 172 privates; wounded were 2 staff officers, 2 captains, 6 subalterns, and 275 privates.

English deaths were 1 captain and 19 privates; 4 officers and 90 privates were wounded.

Enemy deaths were 3 officers and 60 privates, and 10 officers and 100 privates wounded.

Captured artillery amounted to four 32-pound cannons, two 18-pound cannons, seven 12-pound cannons, five 9-pound cannons, fifteen 6-pound cannons, eight 4-pound cannons, and two howitzers, besides considerable munitions.

Our troops earned great honor today, and even more so because this victory, in many respects, was very deceptive and especially however, because the plan had excellent preparations, as the city of New York was completely protected. Our brigade moved back into camp at nine o'clock in the evening, except for the von Mirbach Regiment which had remained behind to escort the prisoners to Harlem and guard them at that place.

Sunday, the 17th of November - Nothing new. I bathed today in the North River. It was very cold..

Monday, the 18th of November - Two Hessian brigades, those of Colonels von Lossberg and von Huyn, marched today from Kingsbridge to near New York, in order to go to Rhode Island, and entered camp near the city until they could be embarked. [Marginal Note - The regiments - Leib, Prince Charles, Wutginau, von Huyn, von Buenau, and von Ditfurth]. My brother, who has not been well for some time and is especially sick at this time, moved into a house close to the road and near New York. Rather good weather.

[Code that I can not decipher.]

Tuesday, the 19th of November - The English brigades still here marched to New York in order to join those embarked for Rhode Island. The brigade of General Stirn remained in the old defenses.

During the afternoon I went hunting, shot a large hare, which looks like our hares, and a few squirrels, which in this land are edible. Hares, or more accurately rabbits, are not plentiful, which is not surprising as every place has been settled by people. There are more partridges but they are too quick.

Wednesday, the 20th of November - Our Grenadiers and Jaegers, the English Grenadiers, light troops, and Scots marched from Kingsbridge under the command of Lieutenant General Milord Cornwallis and were carried across the North River to New Jersey.

The opposite shore, where these troops landed, was surrounded with cliffs of a frightful height. The entire corps had to climb the high cliffs on a small footpath only a few paces wide. The height from the shore to the woods above, which were also surrounded by cliffs, was a bit more than a mile, and several hundred, courageous men, posted on these heights could have held off our entire corps, and could have killed the greatest part. [Marginal Note - The enemy left his guard at Fort Lee and our troops captured them, taking one lieutenant, one quartermaster, three surgeon's mates, and 99 privates prisoner.] The rebels still shaken by the capture of Fort Washington and surprised by the landing of our troops, fled, abandoning another strong fort. This fort lay just opposite Fort Washington and had the name Lee. Our troops found 26 cannons and much ammunition and more than 2,000 tons of the best flour [or possibly powder as the last word is too faded to read.]

Thursday, the 21st of November - Nothing new. Raw weather. On picket duty.

Bardeleben Diary

Friday, the 22nd of November - Everything quite peaceful. Cold weather.

Saturday, the 23rd of November - Nothing new. The same weather. I visited my brother, still down sick.

Sunday, the 24th of November - Nothing new. The 2nd and 4th English Brigades, and the 1st Battalion of the 71st Regiment joined Cornwallis in Jersey. [Marginal Note - Unreadable due to the edge of the page being worn away.]

Monday, the 25th of November - Nothing new. [Marginal Note - General Cornwallis left the region of Fort Lee and went to Hackensack, and made camp on the heights there, today.]

Tuesday, the 26th of November - Nothing new. [Marginal Note - The above mentioned corps continued its march, but because of bad weather today, they were delayed and at evening bivouacked.]

Wednesday, the 27th of November - Nothing new. I rode to my brother and found him to be somewhat better.

Thursday, the 28th of November - Nothing new. General Cornwallis arrived at Newark [NJ] and camped there.

Friday, the 29th of November - Nothing new. Bad weather. Cornwallis arrived at Elizabethtown, which the rebels had left the night before.

Saturday, the 30th of November - Nothing new. The corps arrived at Boundbrook today. [The edge of the page is frayed but it appears that there may have been a marginal note.]

Sunday, the 1st of December - Nothing new. Bright weather. I bathed in the North River. [The edge of the page is frayed but the marginal note seems to translate - General Cornwallis arrived at Brunswick without having made contact with the enemy.] The rebels, who had occupied Brunswick, fired heavily against the corps and planned to defend the river there, as well as the city. However, at evening they abandoned the city. Captain von Weitershausen was wounded.

Bardeleben Diary

Monday, the 2nd of December - Nothing new. Rather cold. Captain von Weitershausen, who was wounded yesterday, died today.

Tuesday, the 3rd of December - Nothing new. I went hunting.

Wednesday, the 4th of December - Nothing new. We received orders to be ready to march into the city tomorrow. Therefore much baggage was sent there today. Good weather.

Thursday, the 5th of December - At nine o'clock this morning our brigade marched into winter quarters in New York. The von Truembach Regiment did the same. It and the Hereditary Prince, by a throw of the dice, entered the barracks. Donop and von Mirbach entered various houses vacated by the rebels. One hundred to 200 men entered each house. The officers remained with their troops as necessary, and they were quartered two to a room. The necessary furniture, such as beds, tables, and benches were provided. Wood, coal, candles, and rather good provisions, also iron pots for cooking, everything necessary, nothing was missing.

Ensign von Trott and I lodged together with our company. Also in the house were Captain Gissot, Captain von Gall, Lieutenant Hausmann, Ensign Freyenhagen, and Lieutenant Keyser of the Artillery, and 100 men. [Marginal Note - The weather today was excellent and just as in summer.]

Friday, the 6th of December - It seemed now as if everything would be quiet. The city is quite secure. The garrison consists of four Hessian and three English regiments. Outside the city, here and there, are more strong contingents of English troops. The Hessian von Truembach, von Stein, and von Wutginau Regiments, and some English regiments are at Kingsbridge, all of whom are in barracks. An English regiment lies at Harlem to cover the East River. [Marginal Note - Our Grenadiers arrived at Boundbrook today, where they found a considerable amount of flour and rum.]

Bardeleben Diary

Saturday, the 7th of December - [Marginal Note - The corps moved out of Boundbrook to Princeton where at evening it had to bivouac.] Nothing new. The Hereditary Prince Regiment furnished the watch today. The city hall serves as the place for the main watch which consists of a captain, two subalterns, and 63 privates. The other posts, of which there are three, consist of 20 to 22 men and have only to watch over magazines. Generally the duty regiment provides about 350 men and the remaining men are assigned picket duty. Each regiment daily provides one captain, two subalterns, and fifty men for the pickets, so that by every alarm they can respond quickly.

Sunday, the 8th of December - [Marginal Note - The corps in Jersey arrived at Trenton. The night before our troops arrived, the enemy crossed the Delaware River, completely evacuating Jersey.] A Reformed and a Lutheran church were made available to us so that we could conduct our religious services.

Monday, the 9th of December - Nothing new.

Tuesday, the 10th of December - The Truembach Regiment marched to Kingsbridge in order to take the place of the Koehler Grenadier Battalion which had crossed into Jersey.

Wednesday, the 11th of December - Nothing new. Sort of cold.

Thursday, the 12th of December - Winter appears to have begun in earnest today. It snowed and froze, although not all that heavy.

Friday, the 13th to the 25th of December - [Marginal Note - Major Hinte, Lieutenants Murhard, von Nagel, Sr., and von Nagel, Jr., and Ensigns von Trott and von Knoblauch are sick.] Nothing new. The weather during this time very changeable, first hail, then snow and rain, but nevertheless, very pleasant and healthy air.

Thursday, the 26th of December - [Marginal Note - The corps in Jersey, which entered winter quarters on the fourteenth of this month, had placed its posts too far apart, in all respects.]

Bardeleben Diary

On the night of the 25th-26th - this Christmas holiday - Rall's Brigade was attacked and almost completely captured. Washington crossed the Delaware with his corps a few miles above Trenton, where the brigade of the von Knyphausen, von Lossberg, and Rall Regiments was quartered. The brigade had to cover the right wing of the corps which had winter quarters in the cities of Princeton, Brunswick, Amboy, Elizabethtown, and Newark. The brigade of Colonel von Donop lay at Bordentown and Burlington, in order, together with Rall's Brigade, to occupy the banks of the Delaware as much as possible. Washington, who during the night, disregarding a really terrible storm with snow and strong hail mixed together, had remained hidden in a woods in order to attack the city before dawn with his full force and to break into it with all his strength. The enemy was so suddenly in the city and posted so quickly before the houses that almost no one was able to take any counter measures. The rebels, with this advantage, at the same time seized the brigade's six cannons and at once put them to their own use, firing heavily against anyone who tried to gather or tried to escape. Colonel Rall was wounded at the start and by his own host, as he came out of the house. Because he continued to live and refused [to surrender], he was stabbed several times with bayonets and quickly died therefrom.

Concerning this unfortunate experience, much has been discussed and criticized. In part it is not, as is now said, proper to have eighteen year-old individuals as the subalterns of the regiment. Still, I prove the advantage which I am to the general officers, staff officers, and captains. Also, I am seen in a favorable way by all my comrades and loved from the heart by the non-commissioned officers and privates.

Due to my fortunate situation, I find more opportunities to experience many things than would otherwise have been possible. However, only the wisest of the wisest Germans can fully understand the peculiar attitude of the English toward the

Bardeleben Diary

Americans. And, therefore, the average uninitiated person of my age and experience understands even less.

Friday, the 27th through the 31st of December - Nothing new. During this time cold, but not very clear weather.

- - - - - - - -

Lieutenant Colonel [William] Harcourt of the King's Dragoons made a patrol into Jersey with thirty of his troops in order to learn the enemy's dispositions. After traveling several English miles, he captured an enemy captain, from whom he extracted various reports, among others, that [the American] General [Charles] Lee was staying in a house about seven miles farther away and had only a guard with him.

Lieutenant Colonel Harcourt marched with his detachment, unmolested, to the house, to which the captured captain had to show the way. As soon as the lieutenant colonel was near the house, he divided his troops into several small groups and rushed the house from all sides. General Lee's adjutant tried to alert the guard but the lieutenant colonel's determination soon caused the guard to flee and General Lee and his adjutant were fortunately taken to Brunswick [on 14 December].

Bardeleben Diary
1777

Wednesday, the 1st of January - That which is considered the essence of politeness in Germany, is completely ignored here.

Thursday, the 2nd to the 17th of January - Nothing of note. Always rather cold. On the fourth of the month fires broke out but did not do much damage.

Saturday, the 18th of January - Already for some time the rebels at Kingsbridge had had this intention [to attack], and almost daily the troops have been seen, and have often risked small raids on our outposts. (They still have hopes of once again capturing Fort Washington.) Early this morning the rebels advanced with a large corps up to the lines at Kingsbridge and called upon one of the main defenses to surrender, with the threat of no mercy if this were not done. Shortly after giving the challenge, the enemy brought up his cannons and a heavy exchange followed. The heavy cannonade from our side, including a few lucky shots, resulted in the loss of one of their cannons and several men, and drove them away, so that they abandoned their appeal for the time being, and sought a complete withdrawal. We lost an artilleryman in the defenses when he was hit by a cannonball.

It appeared the rebels had made their intended effort today because the Queen of England's birthday was to be celebrated with great pomp and ceremony, and already in the morning many of the soldiers were in an unusually drunken condition.

As a result, His Excellency, Lieutenant General Lord [sic] Howe, on this day had made all possible festive preparations to celebrate the event. At eight o'clock this evening, before the house of Lord Howe, a rather large fireworks was displayed. Afterward a ball was held and a grand dinner. All the junior officers were invited to attend these activities, also. However, as most of them were on duty, few could attend. To insure the security of the city, the usual guard on picket duty was

Bardeleben Diary

strengthened by an additional captain, two subalterns, and fifty privates, who had to move out during the evening, and were posted in and outside the city, by Lieutenant Colonel von Schieck, staff officer of the day, in order to keep a watch over the entire city. Although I was free of all duty, I settled for drinking a glass of wine in peace and quiet.

Sunday, the 19th of January - Nothing new. Very cold but not as bad as in Hesse. Mainly the weather seems to be very mild.

Monday, the 20th of January - Nothing new. I went on guard duty.

Tuesday, the 21st of January - At nine o'clock in the evening a fire broke out not far from my quarters. During this alarm it was my fate to lose my sash and some money, about thirty Thalers, and in a most innocent manner. Soon after the fire broke out I sought to bring together the men on picket duty from my quarters, as well as those from other areas, so that when officers to assume command arrived, they would find the troops ready and could march off at once. After this activity, I ran to the fire. As I looked about, and because I noticed no picket had moved out and help was much needed, I returned to see if an officer had arrived. However, the troop was still standing as I had left them. For fear that my commander would be held responsible for their being detained so long, I took the picket, marched to the fire, and directed the necessary action. Still none of the other officers appeared. When the fire was out I first noticed that I had lost my sash and my efforts to find it again were in vain. Most of the sailors from all the ships had been sent to help. This happened whenever there was a fire alarm.

Wednesday, the 22nd of January - Nothing new. I had it announced that I had lost a sash and that the finder would be paid one guinea.

Thursday, the 23rd of January - Several officers had made arrangements to hold meetings twice a week, namely on

Bardeleben Diary

Monday and Thursday and these began today. Several staff and junior officers, English as well as Hessian, voluntarily joined this group and paid for wood and candles, jointly.

Thursday, the 6th of February - Toward evening I went to the East River to shoot ducks. On this venture I nearly lost my life. A bullet flew past my ear, about the width of my hand away, without my being able to determine where it came from. The local inhabitants are still staunch rebels and go out to them almost daily.

Friday, the 7th of February - Nothing new. The cold has eased. The inhabitants can not remember ever having had such a mild winter.

Saturday, the 8th of February - The Combined Battalion of 500 to 600 men, from Rall's Brigade, marched from here to New Jersey today under the command of Lieutenant Colonel von Schieck of the Mirbach Regiment.

Sunday, the 9th to the 13th of January - Nothing new. Mild weather.

Friday the 14th of February - A fire broke out during the afternoon but was quickly extinguished. I was on guard duty today.

Saturday, the 15th of February - Again toward evening there was a fire in the city. As determined as this evil nation is to lay the city in ashes, it does not appear that they will be able to accomplish their goal. The fire-fighting preparations are the very best and at most only one house can be affected by the flames. Mild weather. Mr. Lepner was my guest and we ate at [David] Grimm's house.[17]

Sunday, the 16th of November - Toward evening a fire.

* * * * * * *

17. Mr. Lepner has not been further identified. David Grimm was the owner of an establishment providing food, drinks, and lodgings, and apparently the only such establishment, catering to the Hessians. One of Grimm's daughters, Maria Elisabeth, married Hessian Lieutenant Johann Andreas Karl von Stein zu Altenstein, and another daughter, Peggy, wrote a poem in the autograph book of Captain Christian von Urff of the Hesse-Cassel Leib Regiment.

Bardeleben Diary

A house burned down. At our noon meal we had two English captains as guests. We had our dinner at Grimm's house. I did not eat with these two officers because on several occasions and quite by accident I have skipped such courtesies and - nolens Volens. [I do not know what this means.] These two days cost more than fifteen Thalers.

Monday, the 17th of February - Again a fire. Nothing new today. Rather cold.

Tuesday, the 18th of February - Nothing new. Cold.

Wednesday, the 19th and 20th of February - Nothing new. Very cold.

Friday, the 21st of February - His Excellency, Lieutenant General von Heister, was informed from Kingsbridge that Ensign Cleve of the Truembach Regiment had been stabbed to death by an officer during a social evening; not in a duel, but in an unknown manner.

Today the cold was so severe that a glass of water in my room froze.

Saturday, the 22nd of February - The cold continued just as severe. Otherwise, nothing new.

Sunday, the 23rd of February - Mr. Lepner asked me to dinner yesterday, so I went to his home. Quite pleasant weather.

Monday, the 24th of February - Today I went with Captain Donop on the main watch. During the afternoon and evening there was a fire in the city, which, however, did little damage. Also at nine o'clock in the evening our sentry was fired upon. It was a Negro, who was arrested. It snowed all day.

Tuesday, the 25th of February - It continued to snow throughout the past night and only quit at noon today. The snow was quite deep. During the evening several officers from our regiment and the Hereditary Prince Regiment had a picnic at Grimm's house. I was not among the group.

Wednesday, the 26th of February - Nothing new. Really mild weather. It thawed.

Thursday, the 27th of February - Beautiful weather.

Bardeleben Diary

Friday, the 28th of February to the 3rd of March - Nothing new. Very cold weather and hard freezes.

Tuesday, the 4th of March - Captain Venator and I talked in his quarters. [Code that I can not decipher.]

Wednesday, the 5th of March - I ate at noon with a ship's captain aboard his ship. Clear but cold weather.

Thursday, the 6th of March - I went on guard. It rained and snowed all day.

Friday, the 7th of March - Captain Hamilton and another ship's captain dined with me at noon.

Saturday, the 8th to the 10th of March - Nothing new. Very pleasant and rather warm weather.

Tuesday, the 11th of March - At parade today several officers of our regiment mentioned that reports had been received that my mother was not dead but lay dangerously ill, without hope of recovery. Lieutenant von Nagel, Jr., soon found out for me that Captain Venator had received the report from a friend a few days earlier when a packet boat arrived here and his correspondent had assured him the report was well-founded. A situation which made me uncommonly sick and whose sad images made me mad, but because Captain Venator did not want to tell me this secret., there was nothing more definite that I could discover in this situation; I distrusted all the rumors.

Wednesday, the 12th of March - During the past night Captain [Johann Friedrich Zacharias] Wagner of the von Huyn Regiment, who lay sick here in New York, committed suicide by making two cuts in his neck. The reason for this terrible death is unknown. Exceptionally bad weather. It was foggy and there was lightning toward evening.

Thursday, the 13th and the 14th of March - Nothing new. Pleasant and rather warm weather.

[Code that I can not decipher.]

Saturday, the 15th of March - Because the weather tends to get steadily warmer, we started drilling today. At two o'clock in the afternoon the regiment marched outside the city to some open fields. An ordinary drill by files was held.

Sunday, the 16th of March - At four o'clock in the afternoon I rode to Mr. Lepner's. Pleasant weather.

Monday, the 17th of March - A messenger who had come here with us from Hesse returned with several others from here on some provisions ships returning to England. I took this opportunity to send letters to Hesse, in part several that I had finished writing in February, but had no chance to sent off, and part newly written, namely to Gilsa, to Maischete to my friend von Stuckrod, to Cassel to Lieutenant von Gilsa, also to Cattenbruch and Sippenhausen. I did not leave my quarters all day. Rather warm weather.

Tuesday, the 18th of March - We drilled in the morning. In the afternoon I went horseback riding.

Wednesday, the 19th of March - In the afternoon I went sightseeing. The weather was very pleasant.

Thursday, the 20th of March - It rained all day. [Code that I can not decipher.]

Friday, the 21st of March - Very good weather. In the afternoon I went horseback riding.

Saturday, the 22nd of March - Nothing new. Quite good weather. [Code that I can not decipher.]

Sunday, the 23rd of March - [Code - Captain Gall received a letter.] [Marginal Note - containing information that my mother had died.] that my brother had married Carolina von Gilsa from the establishment at Obernkirch and whose sister Charlotha had taken over the establishment again. Therefore the death of my beloved mother was sufficiently disseminated. Sad in consideration of all the circumstances. So what help is all the worry and to what purpose all the gloomy pictures which thoughts of the future increase? In the future what I can neither see before time nor change, I will leave to God. [Code that I can not decipher.]

Bardeleben Diary

Monday, the 24th of March - At two o'clock in the afternoon Lieutenants Kumell, von Anderson, von Eschwege, von Nagel, Jr., and I went hunting. Lieutenant Eschwege shot a woodcock and I a duck. Many woodcocks are being shot at the present time, in part young ones, however, and that they hatch here is certain because Colonel von Hachenberg's Jaegers shot one on its nest a few days ago.

On our return on most roads we found cattle lying and that only because of a shortage of forage. Above all at the present time the maintenance for cattle is so scarce that many farmers either ship their cattle away or slaughter them. Even food for people is becoming scarce and costs more each day.

Tuesday, the 25th of March - From eight to ten o'clock in the morning the regiment drilled by companies. [Code that I can not decipher.]

Wednesday, the 26th to the 30th of March, at Easter - Nothing new. Rather good weather. [Code that I can not decipher.]

Monday, the 31st of March - An English corps of 500 men under the command of Colonel Byrd embarked here on the North River and departed in the evening. It landed at Peekskill, thirty English miles from New York, where the rebels had established several magazines. The rebels, completely surprised by the unexpected arrival of our troops, took flight after setting some storehouses on fire. This did not prevent the destruction and burning of the following:

    1) 700 barrels of flour
    2) 200 bushels of wheat, a bushels two and one-half pecks
    3) 500 bushels of other grain for cattle
    4) 800 bushels of buckwheat
    5) 300 barrels of rum
    6) 500 weapons
    7) 150 barrels of molasses sugar [sorgum ?]
    8) 250 barrels of flour and pork

In the second storehouse:

Bardeleben Diary

9) 2,500 bushels of wheat
10) 10 barrels of rum
11) 17 barrels of pitch and tar
12) 20 barrels of pork

In addition to this, much was destroyed which could not be used. The value of all this was estimated at about 70,000 pounds sterling. Our troops could take very little of this with them because not far away the enemy had a strong corps. They could not delay, but as soon as their mission was accomplished they had to return to New York.

Not one of our men was lost on this expedition.

I went on guard duty today.

Tuesday, the 1st of April - Nothing new. Raw air.

Wednesday, the 2nd of April - Nothing new, at least in my room. What happens outside of it I am unable to say because I am almost always at home.

Thursday, the 3rd of April - Nothing new. I remained in the house all day. Cold weather.

Friday, the 4th of April - My good friend Lieutenant Berdot of the Landgraf Regiment arrived here yesterday and took lodgings in the Grimm house. I are with him yesterday afternoon and we were pleased to see one another.

Saturday, the 5th of April - At twelve o'clock noon two men were sentenced to death. A soldier who deserted during a skirmish with a troop of rebels but was immediately captured; the other was a sailor who stole. Both of them had taken this well and faced death with considerable courage. Yesterday I had to dine with Berdot at Grimm's house. Rather cold weather.

Sunday, the 6th of April - I came off the guard at the provisions gate. Lieutenant Berdot ate with me and then left during the evening.

Monday, the 7th of April - Berdot was my guest and we ate at Grimm's house.

Bardeleben Diary

Tuesday, the 8th of April - We drilled from eight to ten o'clock in the morning. The weather is already very warm. Lieutenant Berdot returned to Brunswick [NJ] today.

Wednesday, the 9th of April - We drilled this morning from eight to ten o'clock. [Code that I can not decipher.] Very warm. At home in the afternoon.

Thursday, the 10th of April - We drilled today like yesterday. [Code that I can not decipher.] Very warm and almost as hot as in Hesse in high summer.

Friday, the 11th of April - We drilled like yesterday. [Code that I can not decipher] not at home. All afternoon, as usual, I was at home.

Saturday, the 12th of April - There was no drill. Rather good weather. At ten o'clock in the evening Pastor Coester of our regiment, who has been for some time with our Grenadier Battalion, came here from Brunswick and took lodgings with me. Because my bed was too small, we made a bed on the floor.

Sunday, the 13th of April - I went to church. Pastor Coester ate with me.

Monday, the 14th of April - We drilled this morning from eight to ten o'clock. [Code that I can not decipher] officers ate with me.

Tuesday, the 15th of April - Drill continued from eight to ten o'clock. Our regiment did not have to participate as we had the watch today. Ensign von Trott took my tour of duty.

Wednesday, the 16th of April - Nothing new. The pastor ate with me.

Thursday, the 17th of April - We drilled and maneuvered from eight to eleven o'clock. [Code that I can not decipher.]

Friday, the 18th of April - The drill and maneuvering remained as it was yesterday. [Code that I can not decipher.] Pastor Coester did not eat with me. At seven o'clock in the evening there was a small party at Grimm's house. Mr. Grimm had been so good as to have a life-size likeness of our Landgraf made and displayed it as a shield on his home. Today was set

Bardeleben Diary

aside for this celebration. The portrait was hung. We drank a toast to our Prince in silence in the house. Soon the party became noisier. Chaperons and ladies entered and we had a picnic. I was present in this group, and as usual the odd person. I danced, at first alone and then a Scottish quadrille with two young ladies [nymphs]. With them I ended my presence, and it was eight o'clock in the evening when I again returned home.

Saturday, the 19th of April - There was no drill. At nine o'clock in the morning the companies were measured. A rather great number of rebel deserters arrived here today. According to a written proclamation today [Marginal Note - from General Howe], namely that all those who prior to 1 May of this year voluntarily come in, shall, if they bring their weapons, receive not only 24 florins, for each weapon, but also shall have duty [with the English] or their previous freedom.] The pastor ate with me. Yesterday's picket ended at five o'clock this morning.

Sunday, the 20th of April - Our regiment provided the watch today. I had no duty. The pastor ate with Colonel von Gose. I went to church in the morning and otherwise remained at home.

Monday, the 21st of April - At one o'clock in the afternoon the English regiments, lying here in the city and nearby, were embarked on the North River close to New York. No one yet knows where these troops are bound. The three Hessian regiments alone must now provided the services here. The Hereditary Prince Regiment drilled today and the von Mirbach Regiment provided the watch force.

Tuesday, the 22nd of April - From eight to eleven o'clock this morning our regiment drilled. The Hereditary Prince Regiment provided the watch and the von Mirbach Regiment was free. Therefore we maneuvered alone. [Code that I can not decipher.] Pastor Coester ate with me.

Wednesday, the 23rd of April - Our regiment provided the watch. I also had duty with it. At nine o'clock in the morning my guest, Pastor Coester, returned to Brunswick.

Bardeleben Diary

Thursday, the 24th of April - It rained all day. The air was warm and the rain refreshing. I was at home all afternoon. [Code that I can not decipher.]

Friday, the 25th of April - There was no drill. Very good weather. I remained at home. [An illegible word.] I received a letter from Lieutenant Berdot at Brunswick.

Saturday, the 26th of April - Our regiment provided the watch today. I was free. April weather all day. Fate often takes strange twists. A butcher from Germany travels, based on his skills, and fate leads him here to America. Tiring of his profession he becomes a preacher, and finally, with the rebels, a soldier. He demonstrates some ability and presently is a general.[18]

Sunday, the 27th of April - At home all day. I received a letter from Lieutenant Berdot with an inclosed assignation for St. John's Day [25 June], which I should take for my sole use, unasked for, from him. The offer in and of itself had a great appeal to the best friendship and I would be committing an injustice if I did not see it as a proof of his good and unselfish heart. However, as little also as I need to hold this courtesy of my friend for anything less than compulsion, and even though this handling was a result of his noble disposition, at the same time it was completely against my nature to make use of it, or furthermore from this side, to serve what may be considered a full display of friendship. Therefore I respect such a heart and am endlessly pleased when I can find someone of a similar nature.

Monday, the 28th of April - Drill was held from eight to ten o'clock in the morning and just as usual. [Code that I can not decipher.] It was rather cold. I wrote to Lieutenant Berdot in the afternoon and returned his assignation.

Tuesday, the 29th of April - The von Donop Regiment provided the city watch today. I was free; a good friend agreed to take my duty. After guard mount I went home.

Bardeleben Diary

Wednesday, the 30th of April - Nothing new. Cold and raw weather. April ended with much rain.

****

18. Possibly a reference to the American General Peter Muhlenberg, who had served in the Ansbach-Bayreuth military in his youth.

Bardeleben Diary

Thursday, the 1st of May - The corps, consisting of 1,600 men with six cannons, under the command of Generals [William] Tryon and Erskine, which left here on 21 April, returned to their quarters at six o'clock this morning. This detachment, as already mentioned, embarked on 21 April, went up the East River, and landed about six o'clock on the evening of 25 April, near Norwalk. The landing was completed by ten o'clock. The troops marched inland 25 English miles and arrived at Danbury at three o'clock in the afternoon, without having met any resistance. The following day and a part of the next morning was used to destroy the enemy's preparations at that place. At nine o'clock on the morning of 27 April the troops returned from there, boarded ship, and departed from there to continue on to Ridgefield, where they initially encountered a corps of rebels who had constructed defenses at the pass leading to the mentioned city. The rebels had to abandon the defenses after a minimal attack and did nothing to save their established magazines.

After taking all necessary protective measures against the enemy, our troops marched again at four o'clock in the morning of 28 April in order to return to New York. The rebels harassed them on their march and fired heavily against our troops on the flanks and on the rearguard. As the corps halted about half a mile from the ships, a rebel party of about 4,000 men, who everywhere lay behind the stone fences (which surround the fields in that region), delivered a heavy fire. Columns of our troops made a sham attack against them and while this was being carried out, General Erskine, with another part, charged them with fixed bayonets, scattering and massacring them. The troops then rode to the ships and were embarked at once. The losses on this expedition for the English troops consisted of ten privates dead and ten officers and eighty privates wounded.

The following provisions were destroyed at Danbury and other places in Connecticut:

1) A lot of artillery, two of iron

Bardeleben Diary

2) 4,000 kegs of beef and pork
3) 1,000 of flour
4) 100 large kegs of ship's bread
5) 89 kegs of rice
6) 120 kegs and 84 gallons of rum
7) A large supply of wheat and corn, all in piles
8) 30 small kegs of wine
9) 150 kegs of molasses
10) 20 kegs of coffee
11) 15 large cases of medicine
12) 10 kegs of saltpeter
13) 1,020 tents with marquees
14) A number of iron cooking pots
15) A large number of hospital tents
16) Engineer, sapper, and carpenter tools
17) A complete book printing press
18) Tar and tallow
19) 5,000 pairs of shoes and stockings
20) 100 kegs of meal and lots of corn (at Ridgefield)
21) 100 kegs of rum
22) Many wooden crates with weapons
23) Field forges
24) 300 tents

Only a little of this could be taken back to New York because of the hasty retreat.

Fortunately for this corps, nothing hindered their return route, as there would have been no way to rescue them. Immediately after their departure for New York, the rebels received a reinforcement of 4,000 men.

Today was rather pleasant. I went walking after daybreak and found that almost everything was in full bloom.

Friday, the 2nd of May - I went walking very early in the morning. The weather was exceptionally nice. Our regiment provided the watch but I remained free and after parade was at home.

Bardeleben Diary

Saturday, the 3rd of May - Nothing new. Exceptionally good weather. I remained at home all day and did not go out at all.

Sunday, the 4th of May - At ten o'clock in the morning I went to church and otherwise remained at home. It rained continuously all day.

Monday, the 5th of May - At nine o'clock in the morning the von Donop and von Mirbach Regiments marched out for drill and at twelve o'clock noon returned to the city. Rather good weather.

Tuesday, the 6th of May - There was no drill except for recruits, whom I had to train from eight until ten o'clock. The weather was rather good. Otherwise, nothing new.

Wednesday, the 7th of May - The von Donop Regiment provided the city watch today. I was also ordered to the duty. It was foggy all day with occasional rain.

Ascension Day, Thursday, the 8th of May - Nothing new. After dark I remained at home. Rather good weather.

Friday, the 9th of May - Because it rained all day today, there was no drill. I remained at home.

Saturday, the 10th of May - There was no drill. The weather was quite good.

Sunday, the 11th of May - At nine-thirty in the morning we held church parade. I attended the service and was home the rest of the day.

Monday, the 12th of May - The von Donop Regiment provided the city watch. I was not on duty. The Hereditary Prince and Von Mirbach Regiments marched out at nine o'clock in the morning to drill and began firing exercise. Each man received eight cartridges.

Tuesday, the 13th of May - There was no drill today. Rather good weather.

Wednesday, the 14th of May - At nine o'clock in the morning the Hereditary Prince and von Donop Regiments held drill. Each man received eight cartridges for firing. [Code that I can not decipher.]

Thursday, the 15th of May - There was no training. Good weather.

Friday, the 16th of May - Because the weather was miserable today, there was no training.

Saturday, the 17th of May - Donop Regiment had the city watch. I was free. The weather was fair.

Sunday, the 18th of May - (Whitsunday) - At nine-thirty in the morning Whitsunday parade. I went to church. Here, as is customary in Germany, it was decorated with nothing but green boughs. Good weather.

Monday, the 19th of May - (2nd Whitsuntide) - I went to church in the morning. Other than that, at home. Some rain.

Tuesday, the 20th of May - There was no further celebrating today. However, at the same time there was a festive calm and the local inhabitants of the city did no work. We were under orders to conduct training, but as it rained all morning, this was postponed.

Wednesday, the 21st of May - At nine o'clock in the morning the Donop and Mirbach Regiments marched out for drill. Each man was issued twelve rounds of ammunition. Captain [Georg] Krug drilled the Artillery and fired the cannons, also. Good weather. [Code that I can not decipher.]

Thursday, the 22nd of May - The Donop Regiment furnished the city watch today. I was part of it. Exceptionally good weather.

Friday, the 23rd of May - As the Mirbach Regiment relieved us, the Hereditary Prince Regiment drilled alone.

Some English regiments, as well as Hessian regiments, received the order to be prepared to march. [Code - Colonel Block] put off placing [Code - Major Biesenrodt] in house arrest for several days. Today he had a hearing to conduct in this matter, because this thing had many facets, all of which had to

Bardeleben Diary

be well-considered {Code that I can not decipher.] Fair weather.

Saturday, the 24th of May - At nine-thirty in the morning we moved out to drill and because this would be the last time, the flags were taken along. At the edge of the city the regiments loaded [their weapons]. Each man received twelve rounds. Then each marched to the left, then at the drill area counter-marched, formed divisions, and marched in two columns to a certain point; that is the Hereditary Prince Regiment on the right and Donop on the left, (the von Mirbach Regiment had the city watch), then deployed to the left and right, twice by platoons, at that place, twice with the full battalions. In the same manner we turned to the right and advanced an equal number of times. After a brief halt, two battalions were formed from each regiment and a few movements executed, such as passing through (one file through another, counter-marching, and such. [I can not decipher a marginal note in code.]

After all this, as it was one o'clock noon, we marched back to our quarters. The weather was exceptionally good.

Sunday, the 25th of May - I went to church in the morning and remained at home in the afternoon. Very hot weather.

Monday, the 26th of May - I remained at home all day and finished an account of our campaign in the year 1776, which is to be sent to Lieutenant General [Wilhelm Heinrich August] von Donop.

I finally received a letter from Sippenhausen. It had been brought by the packet boat which arrived here yesterday, and was from my sister. She informed me of my mother's death. I only learned that my old father had died shortly thereafter from [Daniel] Schultz, our wagonmaster, who brought the report to me later.

Tuesday, the 27th of May - All the preparations for the new and second campaign were finished. The two English regiments, which had been in winter quarters in the area just outside the city, went aboard ship on the North River. The

Bardeleben Diary

Hessian regiments, including Stirn's Brigade, were to be prepared to embark, also, to collect the heavy baggage, and to assign an officer from the von Donop Regiment to be responsible for it. This morning Colonel von Gose called me to him and gave me the assignment. As it was not my turn for duty and because there were various other duties to which I had been assigned, I sought to avoid this duty by presenting all my reasons, but not because of the duty itself.

Wednesday, the 28th of May - The Leib and Prince Charles Regiments and the English 63rd Regiment arrived here from Rhode Island. During the afternoon Lieutenant General von Heister received information from Kingsbridge that Captain [Georg] Stoebel of the Wissenbach Regiment had committed suicide by cutting his throat, but that the reason was unknown.

The money bonus for every officer from the Crown of England was received today, namely, each colonel [blank] pounds sterling, each lieutenant colonel and major [blank] pounds sterling, each captain twenty pounds, each subaltern eight to twelve shillings.

Thursday, the 29th of May - The three regiments which arrived here from Rhode Island landed and had to enter camp at one of the large resting places outside the city. I went there in the afternoon and visited some of my acquaintances.

Good weather and not too warm.

Friday, the 30th of May - Nothing new. I remained at home all day. Wrote to Sippenhausen, Cattenbruch, and because since the death of my parents, I had received no news of the settlement of the estate, I also wrote to my parents' previous administrator, Dieckmann. Good weather.

Saturday, the 31st of May - This morning the Prince Charles Regiment marched to Kingsbridge. On the other hand, the Leib Regiment remained in camp just outside the city and, because the Hereditary Prince Regiment was rather weak, was assigned to General Stirn's Brigade. Very pleasant weather.

Bardeleben Diary

Sunday, the 1st of June - Our regiment had the city watch. I also had duty with it. Very hot weather.

Monday, the 2nd of June - Nothing new. After the watch was relieved, I remained at home. Very warm.

Tuesday, the 3rd of June - At three o'clock in the afternoon a fleet of sixteen sail entered here. There were some Hessian and English recruits; also two regiments of 1,200 men, of Ansbach on board. [Marginal Note - The Ansbach regiments included a company of jaegers, who are to be mixed with ours.]

At four o'clock in the afternoon I received a completely unexpected visit. Lieutenant Colonel Heymell and Major Hinte were returning from a walk, and as it began to rain just as they were in front of my quarters, in order to avoid the rain, they came into my quarters. I already had a visitor, an English captain that I had met by chance, and all of us enjoyed the taste of an excellent punch.

Wednesday, the 4th of June - It was the King of England's birthday. Therefore at twelve o'clock noon Fort George fired some twelve shots and afterward, at one o'clock, all the warships and several transports fired [their cannons]. At nine o'clock in the evening the entire city was illuminated as proof that all the inhabitants at least gave the appearance of being good subjects of the King.

The firing by the ships, which I watched, was very pleasant to see. After I returned, General Stirn, now and again sent me off to make preparations for the baggage.

Thursday, the 5th of June - Immediately after daybreak the regiments of the Stirn Brigade sent all their heavy baggage to the baggage house where I then had to take care of it. At five o'clock in the morning the above regiments, plus the Leib, von Donop, and von Mirbach Regiments marched to their embarkation, close to the city, on the North River. The departure of the von Donop Regiment was very grievous and disturbing to me, as I was left behind, alone.

Bardeleben Diary

Colonel von Gose took the most profound and cordial sort of departure from me. He gave me his lodgings, which were his permanent winter quarters, containing his living rooms with some furniture therein and which were all the more pleasant for me as all the baggage for the Stirn Brigade lay in his house. He also entrusted to me the keys to all his personal chests, containing more than 150 guineas.

Several English regiments were embarked today also, of which some had gone aboard ship already the previous day. During this afternoon the Hessian jaegers and recruits, who had arrived for the regiments on the third, were disembarked. They were assembled on the usual parade ground here in the city and then mustered in the presence of Generals von Heister and von Knyphausen. Then the assignments were made as to how many men each regiment would receive. After the distribution the recruits were assigned quarters in a church, but had to join their respective regiments the next day. For this reason General Stirn sent me to the regimental commanders on the transport ships with the order that each regiment was to send one officer from each company, and one corporal and two privates to New York tomorrow morning to pick up their recruits. This assignment caused many difficulties as I had no boat to use. However, after many formalities, I finally obtained a boat which took me to Colonel von Wurmb's ship. Because of the darkness of the evening I had to give up the efforts to complete my task. Therefore I returned [to land] at eight o'clock in the evening, made my report, and then went home.

Friday, the 6th of June - In compliance with yesterday's orders, the regiment picked up their recruits and immediately took them aboard ships, all of which lay at anchor. Lieutenant Colonel Heymell honored me this morning with a visit as did Captain Venator, Lieutenants Nagel, Jr., von Lepel, and von Lossberg.

Bardeleben Diary

The two Ansbach regiments were landed and entered camp on Staten Island. I was at home almost the entire day. Very warm.

Saturday, the 7th of June - At two o'clock in the afternoon the troops, which had been embarked for several days, sailed for Jersey in order to join the main corps under Lord Cornwallis. Now that all the preparations have been made, the operations in New Jersey will begin. Generals Lord [sic] Howe, Lieutenant General von Heister, and General Stirn still remain in New York.

During the morning I went to General Stirn on business but the rest of the time I was at home. Warm weather.

Sunday, the 8th of June - The above mentioned troops arrived at Amboy and set up camp a few English [miles] from the city, near the corps which was already there.

The united troops now at Amboy consist of the 42nd and 71st Regiments of Scots, the latter contains three battalions, the 4th, 10th, 15th, 17th, 23rd, 27th, 35th, 38th, 40th, 44th, 46th, 55th, and 64th English Infantry Regiments. Also the 17th Dragoon Regiment, Stirn's Brigade, and the Combined Battalion under Colonel [Johann August von] Loos, and the Waldeck Regiment.

The listed troops are camped on the heights near the Sound to the banks of the Raritan River.

The corps of General Cornwallis consists of two Hessian Jaeger Companies, two battalions of English Light Infantry, four battalions of Hessian Grenadiers, including the Koehler Grenadier Battalion, two battalions of Guards from the 5th, 7th, 26th, 33rd, 37th, 49th, and 52nd English Infantry Regiments. In part this corps was camped from the far side of the Brunswick to the Raritan, and the Jaegers are on this side of the Raritan and the two battalions of Guards are on the heights behind them, which allows the road to Bonnington to be kept open.

General Washington now has taken positions from Elizabethtown to Boundbrook, and his army consists of about

Bardeleben Diary

12,000 to 14,000 men, who are in the so-called Blue Mountains near Boundbrook.

It rained all day. I remained at home all day. During the evening I went to Grimm's house, drank a bottle of Scottish ale, and then returned to my lodgings.

Monday, the 9th of June - Lieutenant Generals Howe and von Heister went to join the army in Jersey. In the morning I went to the War Cashier Schmid and drew the pay for my men; then I returned home at once. It rained all day.

Tuesday, the 10th of June - Nothing new. Very warm. I stayed at home all day. At eight o'clock in the evening I bathed in the North River just behind my quarters.

Wednesday, the 11th of June - The 71st and 42nd Regiments of Scots with the Combined Battalion moved closer to Brunswick. The latter camped this side of Brunswick and the first two near Bonnington.

The two Ansbach regiments were sent to Amboy from Staten Island and camped there.

During the evening a transport of baggage arrived from the Leib Regiment. I put it with the other baggage for which I was responsible.

I remained at home all day and finished a few reports for Lieutenant Colonel [Friedrich Ludwig] von Minnigerode, Captain von Eschwege, Lieutenant Freyenhagen, and Pastor Coester. I sent letters, which had arrived a few days ago from Hesse and which I had taken the responsibility to deliver, to the first two. With this opportunity I had the politeness to write.

Thursday, the 12th of June At three o'clock in the morning Lieutenant General von Heister moved out from Amboy with the following regiments: [Marginal Note - and Major Generals Stirn, [Charles] Grey, [John] Vaughan, and Brigadier General [James] Agnew, the Dragoons on foot, Ansbach and English Jaegers, the 17th Dragoon Regiment, mounted, Stirn's Brigade, the 4th, 44th, 15th, 17th, 64th, 38yh, 27th, 10th, 23rd, and 40th English Regiments, as well as twelve light 12-pound cannons and the Queen's Rangers, who covered the flanks.]

This corps marched to Brunswick and camped from this side of Becker's Mill to Bonnington in single camps. Upon the approach of the mentioned corps, the Combined Battalion and the two Hessian Jaeger Companies joined the corps of General Cornwallis beyond Brunswick.

The two Ansbach regiments, the Waldeck Regiment, and the 55th Regiment remained at Amboy to maintain communications between Brunswick and Amboy. The two Ansbach battalions moved to the left and entered camp along the banks of the Raritan. The Waldeck Regiment occupied heights above Amboy on the Sound, and the 55th Regiment moved farther forward so as to be able to observe the road to Woodbridge.

The Commanding General, Lord Howe, arranged the English regiments in New Jersey in the following brigades:

The 1st Brigade, under Lieutenant Colonel Trelawney, consisted of one battalion of Guards and the 23rd and 40th Regiments.

The 3rd Brigade, under Lieutenant Colonel Markham, consisted of the 10th, 27th, and 46th Regiments. Both of these brigades were commanded by General Vaughan.

The 2nd Brigade, under Brigadier General Agnew, consisted of the 4th, 15th, and 44th Regiments.

The 4th Brigade, under Lieutenant Colonel [Charles] Mawhood, consisted of the 17th, 38th, and 64th Regiments. [Marginal Note - Both under the orders of Major General Grey.]

The 5th Brigade, under General Leslie, consisted of the 71st Regiment of Scots containing 3 battalions.

The 6th Brigade, under General [Edward] Mathew, consisted of one battalion of Guards, and the 7th and 26th Regiments.

All these brigades made up the main army.

Bardeleben Diary

Lord Cornwallis' Corps consisted of the following regiments:

1st Brigade, under Lieutenant Colonel [Thomas] Stirling, with the 33rd and 42nd Regiments.

2nd Brigade, Under Lieutenant Colonel Calder, with the 5th, 49th, 52nd, and 37th Regiments.

I remained at home all day and organized the baggage which was still coming in.

I received a letter, among others written to me, from Brunswick that on the sixth of this month a spy was hanged who had exchanged letters with a rebel general, and who sought to get an English grenadier to desert. This spy tried by so many means to get an English grenadier to come over to him, that finally he believed the grenadier to be his friend and confidant. The spy gave him a letter to take to a rebel general which contained information that at present Brunswick was so weakly occupied that it would not take much effort to capture it. And, to make even more certain that it would be captured, the spy, as soon as he heard of the pending attack, would set fire to the city. During the alarm, which would cause everyone to be fully occupied, the city could be attacked.

However, the grenadier so was conscientious that as soon as he discovered the intent, he reported it.

The spy supposedly died in the most noble manner and his death had been celebrated as a sacrifice for freedom, that is, at the gallows he said, "I die for liberty, and do it gladly, because my cause is just."

It rained during the past night and this morning.

Friday, the 13th of June - Nothing new. The weather today was rather raw, but without rain. I wrote to Colonel von Wurmb concerning the latest baggage to arrive.

During the afternoon I visited Lieutenant Schotten and later went for a walk.

Saturday, the 14th of June - During the past night the army at Brunswick had to strike their tents and form two columns with the intent of drawing nearer to the enemy, who was in camp at Boundbrook.

Lord Cornwallis' column marched in the following order: the Hessian and Ansbach Jaegers, two battalions of English Light Infantry, of which however, four companies under Major Gray had to be transferred to Lieutenant Colonel Twisleton, the English Grenadiers, Lieutenant Colonel Stirling's Brigade, Lieutenant Colonel Calder's Brigade, the Hessian Grenadiers, the 16th Dragoon Regiment, of which one officer and sixteen men remained in Brunswick, two light 12-pound cannons and four 6-pound cannons.

General Von Heister's column, with Generals Stirn, Vaughan, Grey, and Brigadier Generals Agnew and Leslie, followed the other column with four companies of Light Infantry under Major Gray, the Light Infantry Company of the Guards with the English Jaeger Company, all under the command of Lieutenant Colonel Twisleton, a corps of pioneers, Lieutenant Colonel Trelawney's Brigade, Stirn's Brigade, the 2nd, 4th, and 3rd Brigades, which have two light 12-pound cannons, and eight 6-pound cannons with them, the 17th Dragoon Regiment, mounted and on foot.

General Leslie's Brigade had the lead and followed immediately behind General Cornwallis.

The regiments left their tents and baggage behind and were allowed to take only two wagons per battalion for the provisions and to carry the officers who were at the head of each brigade.

In addition to these wagons, the army had 300 others loaded with salted meat and rum, which traveled between the columns.

General Mathew's Brigade remained behind with the 7th English Regiment, the Combined Battalion, and the Koehler Grenadier Battalion to cover Brunswick.

At eleven o'clock yesterday evening the army set out in the previously described order and marched along the road to Princeton. After two hours it had to halt before everyone had begun to march. Because the enemy had destroyed the bridge near Kingston and the bridge near Rocky Hills over the Millstone River, the first column had to move farther to the right and take the road over Middlebush to Hillsborough, where they arrived unhindered, after a two hour march [Marginal Note - at ten o'clock this morning] and camped there. The right wing stretched along the Millstone River and above Hillsborough formed an angle.

Captain [Karl August von] Wreden with the 1st Jaeger Company and a part of the Ansbach Jaegers was posted forward where the abatis began, and Captain [Johann] Ewald and the remaining jaegers on the left to cover that flank.

The pickets of this column formed the chain between both Jaeger Companies and extended as far as the bank of the Millstone River.

The enemy had strong detachments in the woods, which lay before this column. They moved these detachments toward the main picket on the left, from which an officer and thirty men were detached to both the left and right. The enemy moved forward to attack these two posts with about 200 men and because the mentioned detachments were in danger, they were pulled back a short way and at the same time, the captain of the main picket moved forward to support them, driving the enemy back again. Two grenadiers of the Minnigerode Grenadier Battalion were wounded during this action.

The second column moved along the road to Hillsborough to Middlebush in Somerset County and took the left road through this place while the Guard Battalion with the Light Infantry and also the English Jaeger Company followed on the road to Brunswick. The von Donop and the von Mirbach Regiments had formed a straight line. The Leib Regiment formed a blunt angle to this road, which from there on made the flank with the English regiments to the 64th Regiment. The second line connected with the first and had a front toward Princeton, which then ran over Middlebush through the 71st

Regiment of Scots, behind which stood the 17th Dragoon Regiment, the Artillery, the Engineers, and the Pioneer Corps, and joined the first line, and with this column formed a five-sided angle. In addition the 4th Regiment was so posted on the road to Boundbrook that the left wing had its pickets joined with those of the Leib Regiment on the right wing and also an abatis.

The English Jaegers with the Light Infantry covered the left flank and that of the 4th Regiment between which they were joined with the pickets of the other regiments of the first line and covered the right flank.

The pickets of the 64th Regiment and those of the other lines, according to the way they were camped, were placed a half mile ahead of their front.

At eight o'clock this morning I went to Major [Carl Leopold] Baurmeister and had tea with him. Next I visited Lieutenant Colonel [Johann Friedrich von] Cochenhausen and then returned home.

I visited Mr. Lepner toward five o'clock in the evening and had tea with him. After remaining there briefly I went to the camp of the Hereditary Prince Regiment where I remained until dusk. On my way home I spoke with Dr. [Karl] Eskuche. We ate dinner together and also with several other clerics and an Ansbach doctor. At ten o'clock I was back in my quarters.

Rather warm weather.

Sunday, the 15th of June - A jaeger patrol had to check out several houses lying just before our front, to see if any rebels were therein. When they approached the houses they were attacked by about 200 men who stormed out of the houses. The rebels were driven back into the woods as a result of the jaegers being reinforced. During this affair our patrol suffered one wounded, one captured, and one surgeon's mate wounded.

Because the army remained standing and did not move forward, those in camp in the region of Middlebush had to send a detachment of 140 men from the 40th Regiment, two

Bardeleben Diary

companies of the 17th Dragoon Regiment, and the English Jaeger Company, and 100 wagons to Brunswick to pick up provisions for the army.

- - - - - - -

I went to church in the morning and after it ended at ten o'clock, I paid my respects to Colonel Block, who because of his sickly condition had returned here this morning.

At three o'clock in the afternoon Dr. Eskuche and Pastor [Johann Georg] Hausknecht visited me, drank coffee with me, and soon thereafter departed again. After they left, two officers came, a Scottish lieutenant and a captain from a warship. I had never spoken to the latter and had only seen the first one passing on the street a few times. As he, however, because all his countrymen dislike us Hessians, seemed very friendly and wanted to convince me otherwise, and had brought along this captain who was also a Scot, we drank several bottles and steins and toward evening I was again alone.

It rained all afternoon rather hard.

Monday, the 16th of June - In Jersey everything remained quiet and the positions were not changed.

Again today 100 wagons left for Brunswick under cover of a strong English escort in order to pick up the army's provisions.

- - - - - - -

I went walking between two and three o'clock this afternoon and otherwise remained at home.

At four o'clock in the afternoon a terrible weather set in and continued for three hours with the strongest rain gust. Fortunately it passed by, however, without doing any damage.

Tuesday, the 17th of June - Our army in Jersey still finds itself in the same situation and everything is quiet.

A packet boat arrived late yesterday evening, bringing many letters from Hesse. However, although almost everyone received a letter, I was not lucky enough to get one.

Late this evening a Hessian Jaeger transport arrived, but one ship with sixty jaegers has fallen into enemy hands.

Bardeleben Diary

Quite good weather. I was at home all day.

Wednesday, the 18th of June - At daybreak an enemy corps moved against the left flank of Cornwallis' Corps. The farthest forward pickets of the Hessian Grenadiers immediately sent out a patrol to reconnoiter the enemy. This patrol had hardly neared the woods on our front when the rebels came out of the same. The rebels would have surrounded our pickets if a jaeger company, with an amusette, had not come to their help fortunately and driven the enemy back with their fire. The rebels fled back into the woods. We had two subalterns and one private killed, three grenadiers and two jaegers wounded, the latter being captured by the enemy. Otherwise the army remained quiet.

During the afternoon I went into the city for a short time after several tours of guard duty, which was held by the Hereditary Prince Regiment today. The rest of the time I was at home.

At twelve o'clock noon the 300 Hessian jaegers who arrived here day before yesterday sailed for Jersey.

Thursday, the 19th of June - Because the enemy would not leave the so-called Blue Mountains near Boundbrook, which were fortified, and would not let us enter them under any conditions, and as nothing could be undertaken against the enemy in his present position, our army left its position to attempt a different approach. Therefore, at daybreak, the army had to move out and formed into two columns. Lieutenant General von Heister's column took the lead and began the march an hour before the other [column]. Previously, however, the 23rd and 40th Regiments had to march half way to Brunswick to secure posts there.

The Light Infantry with the English Jaegers, under the command of Lieutenant Colonel Twisleton, covered the right flank and the 71st Regiment the left flank. The column itself marched in the following order: The Grenadier Company of the Guards, the Guard Battalion, the 3rd Brigade, the 4th Brigade, the 2nd Brigade, whose two regiments, that is, the 23rd and 40th Regiments, then closed with the column.

The Stirn Brigade with the Cavalry and all the pickets.

The baggage wagons went in front of their brigades and of the munitions and provisions wagons, part were at the head of the column, part on the side, on the right flank of the light corps under Lieutenant Colonel Twisleton. After a half hour march the column halted long enough for the 2nd column to close up while Lieutenant Colonel Stirling's Brigade covered both flanks.

Lieutenant Colonel Calder's Brigade was in the lead followed by the Hessian Grenadiers, then the English Grenadiers. The English Light Infantry and the Hessian Jaegers formed the rearguard. The wagons were as divided by the other column.

During the withdrawal of these two columns, small detachments of the enemy were seen occasionally, which also fired, but from a great distance, on the rearguard. However they did nothing more and the army arrived unhindered at Brunswick.

Lord Cornwallis' column camped, part on this side, part on the other side of Brunswick, and the Jaegers took post beside the Minnigerode Brigade on the road to Boundbrook, and in such a manner that they had the Raritan on the left flank.

In New York nothing new. Good weather and quite hot. I went for a short walk along the North River during the afternoon and otherwise I spent the rest of the day at home.

Friday, the 20th of June - In Jersey everything remained quiet and no more enemies were seen, except for single troops who approached our pickets, but at a great distance. Our pickets were set out on this side of the Raritan behind the Jaeger, a few hundred yards from the sentries, as far as Bonnington.

The munitions wagons with the pontoons and the flat boats went to Amboy under the escort of the 31st, 38th, and 52nd Regiments, and the 17th Dragoon Regiment. All the sick were escorted to Brunswick in order to sail to Amboy on the ships lying there.

- - - - - - - -

After the noon meal I went up the East River for an hour and because it was rather hot, I then bathed, but was back home again by five o'clock in the afternoon.

This afternoon evil rebel sympathizers set fire to a house for straw, wood, and similar items, quite near my lodgings. According to their plans, this would have broken out at night. However, because the material for starting the fire was too strong, when placed in the stored items, it was discovered early and extinguished.

Saturday, the 21st of June - In Jersey everything remained quiet and the army continued in place at Brunswick, except that the Koehler Grenadier Battalion marched to Amboy this morning.

- - - - - - - -

At five o'clock this morning I went for an hour's walk along the North River and then returned home. At nine o'clock in the morning I paid my compliments to Colonel [Karl Wilhelm von] Hachenberg in his quarters. At four o'clock in the afternoon I visited Captain [Johann Kaspar] Kuemmel, briefly, who, because the Hereditary Prince Regiment had the city watch today, had the main watch. Otherwise I was always at home.

Sunday, the 22nd of June - Because the enemy's positions were too advantageous and the operations in Jersey could not be continued, the Commanding General Howe decided to leave the area. Therefore, at four o'clock this morning the army left the region of Brunswick and moved to Amboy with the intent of withdrawing the troops as soon as possible to Staten Island, where they are then to embark aboard ship for another destination.

Chaiplains did not wear a uniform; they wore a black suit with a clerical collar. (Photograph by Hans Bleckwenn, 1984 Die Friderizinchen Uniformen, Band Technischen Truppen, Rueckwaertige Dienst und Kiegsformation, Biblio-Verlag, Osnabrueck, Germany.)

The Church Book of Georg Christoph Coester

Chaplain of the Hesse-Cassel von Donop Regiment

Coester's Church Book
Georg Christoph Coester

Georg Christoph Coester was apparently born in late 1751 as his baptism occurred on 15 December 1751. He was the son of Johann Christoph Coester, pastor at Ersen, near Hofgeismar, and his wife Anna Margarete, daughter of Pastor Mathias Weete of Breuna, near Ziernberg. He began his studies for the clergy at Marburg on 17 April 1771 and became chaplain of the von Donop Regiment in 1776 when it was preparing to depart for America.

After eight years of service with the regiment in America, he was on pension for two years and then designated as pastor at Malsfeld in 1786. On 1 May 1787 he married his cousin, Dorothea Wilhelmina Coester, daughter of Pastor Christoph Heinrich Coester of Oberlistingen. Two children, Georg Christoph Bernhard and Heinrich Wilhelm, were born to the couple, the latter of whom also became a pastor.

Georg Christoph Coester died 14 July 1790 at Malsfeld, age 38.

His wartime church book recorded marriages, baptisms, deaths, and even confirmations and penances. Marriages were performed already in Germany. The first baptism took place aboard the transport *Jenny*, en route to America.. Lieutenant Johann Heinrich von Bardeleben was one of the infant's sponsors. (See the Anonymous Hesse-Cassel Diary which precedes this church book.) Mother and child died the following year.

[The above information was extracted from a much longer article written by Walteri Bergman, apparently in 1969, as a supplement to a Melsungen, Germany, magazine, and "The Diary of Chaplain G.C. Coester, 1776-1784", *Geschichtliche Nachrichten aus Treysa*, Reproduced by A. Giebel, A. Helwig, and H. Krause, 1969.]

Coester's Church Book
Introduction

Two articles from German publications, Walteri Bergmann's "Hessische Soldaten als britische Soeldner in den USA (1776-1783)" *Ein Beitrag zur Heimatgeschichte z.Z. der amerikanischen Freiheitskriege nach dem kirchlichen Protocollbuch des Feldpredigers Ch. Coester (Malsfeld) und anderen Melsunger Archivalien, (Melsungen, 1969)* and *Geschichtliche Nachrichten Aus Treysa* containing the Diary of Chaplain G. C. Coester, produced by A. Giebel, A. Helwig, and H. Krause (Treysa, 1969) provide information on the dress and duties of Hesse-Cassel chaplains, as well as a list of the men who served in that role for those troops.

Hesse-Cassel had an area of only 156 square miles and a population of 300,000 citizens. The ruler, Friedrich II, had married a daughter of King George II of England, and in 1762 had abolished the voluntary recruiting system, replacing it with the Prussian canton system, in which each canton was required to supply a predetermined number of recruits for designated regiments. The peacetime army for Hesse-Cassel consisted of only 16,000; fewer than the total supplied to England during the American Revolution. Every tenth man, or every fourth man capable of bearing arms, was sent to America.

To provide chaplains for the various regiments being sent to America, Hesse-Cassel recruited young, recently graduated theologians, who earned their livelihood by tutoring and each of whom was generally assigned to administer religious functions for two regiments. The chaplains were considered as military personnel but wore no uniform. Instead they wore the native Hessian civilian dress worn by the clergy, a black cap or hat, a black coat, and at times, black boots. (See the illustration taken from Hans Bleckwenn, "Die frederizanischen Uniformen", *Technische Truppen, Rueckwaertige Dienste und Kriegsformationen*, Biblio-Verlag, (Osnabrueck, 1984.) They were paid the equivalent of about 100 - 1969 Deutsch Marks, plus ration money for themselves and their servants and forage money. They also received an officer's share of the booty.

Although the latter reference noted that Chaplains Waldeck, of the Waldeck Regiment, and Melsheimer of the Brunswick troops were wounded, I have found no information to confirm that statement.

The chaplains conducted religious services, duty for the troops, on Sundays, and led prayer meetings twice a week, on Tuesday and Friday. The church prayer for both Lutherans and Reformed was as follows:

"We ask you to watch over the rulers of the earth, whom you have sent to rule over us. Take the British King and the entire royal family under your protection. Bless his reign, give success to his plans and undertakings, bless his forces against his enemies, and crown them with the desired good fortune and blessing. Protect the Prince of our land and the entire Hessian ruling house, and send your blessings from on high. Great Jehovah, from whom the holy power, good council, and righteous strength comes, be with us and do not forsake us. Stand by us and especially safeguard our commanding general, bless his plans and undertakings. Also take into your protection our entire general staff, the staff and other officers, privates, and all those who belong to this regiment."

The church books maintained by the chaplains were considered their private property and most have been lost over the years, only those Hesse-Cassel church books of Coester and Kuemmell are known to exist at the present time. In the books marriages, baptisms, deaths, confirmations, and penances were recorded, just as in the church books of the pastors in Germany.

According to August Woringer, cited in the above mentioned articles, the following chaplains served the Hesse-Cassel soldiers in America during the period 1776-1783:

Wilhelm Bauer, from Alt Morschen, matriculated at Marburg 25 October 1770. In 1776 he was assigned to the Knyphausen and Lossberg Regiments. He was captured at

Trenton in December 1776, rejoining his unit after being exchanged. He went to Canada with those regiments in 1780 and returned to Germany with the Lossberg Regiment in 1783. From 1786 to 1814 he was the Reformed pastor in Goershausen.

Friedrich Becker was the son of the garrison chaplain Peter Becker in Carlshafen and his wife, the daughter of the doctor of medicine Ebert in Marburg. He accompanied a recruit transport to America and was assigned as a Reformed chaplain with the Donop Regiment.

Karl Becker brother of Friedrich, was the staff chaplain in 1776 and chaplain of the large Hessian hospital on Long Island in 1782. After the war he became pastor of the Reformed church in Bornich, near St. Goarshausen. In 1831 his widow Sophie Louise, nee Hildebrand, requested the Hesse-Cassel legislature to pay credits owed her husband, but was refused.

Johann Wilhelm Bigel, from Kassel, matriculated at Marburg 18 October 1759. In 1776 he was the Reformed staff chaplain, and served in the campaigns until 1781. He became pastor at St. Goar in 1781 and Reformed inspector on 28 March 1786, and at Nastaetten on 9 March 1801. He died at Nastaetten on 25 October 1815.

Georg Christoph Coester (see biographical sketch as author of his church book.)

Johann Christoph Eskucke was the son of the pastor and professor Balthasar Ludwig Eskucke in Rinteln and his wife Catherina Florentine, nee Faucher. Born 25 May 1751 in Rinteln, he studied in Rinteln, Goettingen, and after 11 May 1773, in Marburg. Assigned as the Lutheran chaplain of the Mirbach Regiment in 1776, he died on 19 May of that year at Bremerlehe, prior to embarking for America.

Johann Conrad Grimmel, son of the merchant Martin Grimmel in Cassel and his wife Anna Catherina Elisabeth, nee Eskucke, was born on 8 September 1753 at Cassel. He matriculated at Marburg on 2 July 1774 and was assigned as Reformed chaplain of the Wiessenbach Garrison Regiment in

Coester's Church Book

1776. From 1784 to 1789 he was second pastor in Ziegenhaim. He married Anna Juliana Grimmel at Ziegenhain on 26 December 1784 and died 26 June 1789 at the age of 34.

Johann Georg Hausknecht, son of Johann Wilhelm Hausknecht, who was in Hessian service, was born 18 October 1750. He matriculated at Marburg on 11 April 1768 and was assigned to the Hereditary Prince Regiment in 1776. Captured at Yorktown in 1781, he was paroled to New York. In 1784 he was named pastor and court chaplain at Philippsthal, and in 1785 pastor of Bockenheim, where the German Reformed District of Frankfurt am Main was headquartered. In 1786 he was pastor in the District of Frankfurt am Main and consistorial councilor. He died 2 December 1812. On 15 June 1790 he had married Christine Maria Anna Krafft, from Kassel, at Frankfurt am Main. She had been born in 1760, the daughter of pastor Justus Christoph Krafft, and died at Hanau on 30 September 1850.

(Possibly Georg Friedrich) Heller, a staff chaplain, was the son of Johann Georg Heller of Fambach, near Schmalkalden, and Martha Elisabeth, nee Loeber.

Johann Henrich Koehler about whom no additional information is available.

Henrich Kuemmell was born 6 December 1753, the son of Adam Friedrich Kuemmell, second pastor at Vacha, and his wife, Christine Charlotta, nee Bodenstein. He matriculated at Rinteln in 1771 and at Marburg on 20 April 1774. He served as chaplain of the Huyn and Buenau Regiments throughout the war, and in 1784 became second pastor of the Reformed Schmalkalden District. In 1803 he was named inspector of the Reformed Church and School of the District of Schmalkalden, and also castle and first pastor of the Reformed District. He died 17 December 1830. On 15 February 1788 he married Christina Margaretha Reimann at Herrenbreitungen. She was born 8 February 1764 in Herrenbreitungen, the daughter of Reformed pastor Georg Philipp Reimann at Herrenbreitungen. She died 22 July 1827 at Schmalkalden.

Coester's Church Book

Johann Konrad Henrich Schrecker, the son of Pastor Henrich Schrecker in Schmalkalden, was confirmed (normally at age 14) at Easter 1761. He served as an assistant in Heinebeck from 1771 to 1776, and became a chaplain in 1776. He died 30 June 1785 at the age of 47 years, 11 months, having previously served as the chaplain for the field hospital chaplain with the Hessian Corps in America.

Georg Christian Stern, son of the First Forest Secretary in Marburg, matriculated at Marburg on 22 March 1764 and 31 March 1768. In 1776 he became a military chaplain. In 1784 he was a deacon in Melsungen and in 1789 the pastor at Nordhausen. He committed suicide 28 November 1793 by jumping into the Fulda River due to melancholy. On 15 September 1784 he married Wilhelmina Juliana Wiesler, who died in November 1798 at the age of 31 and 1/2 years. She was the daughter of the court gardener Johannes Wiesler in the Karlsaue (Karl's Garden) at Kassel.

Rudolf Reinhard Virnau, born 5 January 1749 in Wellershausen, was the son of the local teacher Johannes Virnau and Anna Margaretha, nee Beyer, living in Wellershausen. He matriculated at Marburg on 16 April 1768 and served as rector in Felsberg in 1771. Named chaplain to the Rall and Mirbach Regiments in 1776, he served throughout the war. In April 1784 he became pastor in Sachsenhausen, District of Ziegenhain He died there of a high fever on 21 May 1785. He Married Wilhelmina Peffer of Marburg.

Johann Christoph Weidemann, born 19 September 1751 at Kassel, was the son of the Court Clerk Johann Wilhelm Weidemann and Anna Catherina, nee Hundeshagen. He matriculated at Marburg on 26 June 1770. In 1779 he was the chaplain with the Leib Regiment and served as such until the end of the war. He died at New York. During the crossing to America, his brother, a free corporal of the same regiment, was reported missing.

Coester Church Book
**Born and Baptized
of the Illustrious von Donop Regiment
During the Time I [George Christian Coester]
Served as Chaplain**

Hamilton Carl Heinrich Haemer - Johannes Haemer's, musketeer in the Lieutenant Colonel's Company, legitimate son, was born to Maria Elisabeth Haemer, nee Lohr, on 23 March 1776 at three o'clock in the morning on our trip to America, on the Atlantic Ocean, aboard the English transport ship *Jenny*. The ship's captain, William Hamilton, Lieutenant Colonel [Karl Philipp] Heymell, and Lieutenant [Johann Heinrich] von Bardeleben were asked to be sponsors. The ship's captain was the first, but because he was a Scotsman and a Presbyterian, he did not wish to hold the child to be baptized. His excuse was that it was not customary in his country, and second, as he was always at sea he could not fill the duty which a sponsor has. This excuse seemed valid to us. Lieutenant Colonel Heymell therefore held the child to be baptized and gave the child the name Hamilton Karl Heinrich. The name Hamilton it received from the ship's captain, over his objections, because he said if he should get to Hesse, or if the child came to England, I will recognize his name and then I will take care of him. This festive occasion was conducted while the sea was rather calm on the following day, the 24th of March. He was the first child that I baptized and possibly the first Hessian to be baptized aboard a transport ship on the Atlantic Ocean.

N.B. - The child and his mother died in the autumn of 1777.

Robert Scheffer - born to Johann Henrich Scheffer, corporal in Major von Hinte's Company, and Elisabeth Scheffer, during the night of 11-12 July 1776, on the voyage to America, on the English transport ship *Hope*. Because we had good weather and calm seas on 16 July, I was taken across in a small boat. I baptized him. Robert Peacock, captain of the ship *Hope* held it to be baptized.

Coester Church Book

Arietha Martha Elisabeth - born to Christoph Abel, musketeer in the von Donop Regiment, and his wife Anna Catharina, nee Martin, a daughter, on 12 July during our voyage from Halifax to New York, on the English transport ship *Empress*, and was baptized in my presence by Chaplain Hausknecht of the Hereditary Prince Regiment. The sponsor was Martha Elisabeth, wife of Quartermaster Sergeant Henrich Philipp Roemer of that regiment. The baptism took place on 2 August 1776.

Catharina Elisabeth - a daughter, was born to Johannes Scheffer, musketeer in Colonel von Gose's Company of the von Donop Regiment, and his wife Anna Elisabeth, nee Herd, from Roemersfeld, District of Borken, on 9 October 1776 on the island of New York [Manhattan], in the camp at Bloomingdale, at three o'clock in the morning and baptized the following day, 10 October. The sponsor was Catharina Elisabeth, wife of Corporal Johann Hassenpflug of Colonel von Gose's Company.

N.B. - Died at New York 19 September 1783.

Catharina Elisabeth - illegitimate daughter of Musketeer Adam Sustmann, of Colonel von Gose's Company, born at Wabern, and Maria Elisabeth Wiederhold, born at Gudenborn, District of Borken, on 6 November 1776, at seven o'clock in the evening in the camp on the island of New York, and baptized on the ninth of the month. The sponsor was Caterina Elisabeth, wife of Corporal Johann Hassenpflug of Colonel von Gose's Company.

N.B. - The woman, left behind, I do not know why, by her intended husband, who had promised marriage, had followed. She arrived with the second fleet, sought out her husband-to-be, and, as she set her first foot in his tent, gave birth to a young daughter.

N.B. - Died at Philadelphia.

Johann Adam - son of Joachim Kurz, musketeer in Captain von Kutzleben's Company, and his wife Anna Catharina, nee Viemann, of Zimmersrode, District of Borken, was born between eight and nine o'clock in the evening on 18 December 1776, in our winter quarters in the city of New York. I baptized him on 19 December. The sponsor was Adam Schmeck, drummer of the regiment.

Johannes - son of Adam Schmeck, drummer of Colonel von Gose's Company, and his wife Anna Martha, was born on the night of 30 December in our winter quarters at New York, and baptized on 2 January 1777. The sponsor was Johannes Lumpe, who had been the servant of Captain [Friedrich Karl] von Weitershausen.

N.B. - On 8 January 1777 I was transferred to the von Donop Brigade by His Excellency, Lieutenant General [Leopold] von Heister. The first child I baptized was:

Johann Georg - son of Grenadier Abel Trumpf, of Wolfsanger, District of Kassel and his wife Anna Christina, of Sondershausen, District of Kassel, who was born at four o'clock in the afternoon on 24 January 1777 at New Brunswick in New Jersey in America. I baptized him on 26 January 1777. Sponsor was Johann Georg Schwarz, a grenadier in the Leib Regiment, born in Weninzenhausen

Anna Catherina - legitimate daughter of Johann Henrich Otto, grenadier in Lieutenant Colonel von Minnigerode's Battalion, and his wife Angelica Dorothea Stark, born at Grebenstein, was born at four o'clock in the morning on 29 January 1777 at New Brunswick in the province of New Jersey, and baptized there on 31 January 1777. Sponsor Anna Catherina, wife of Johann Krueck, grenadier in the same battalion.

Catherina Elisabeth = legitimate daughter of Grenadier Johannes Schmidt, of the Koehler Grenadier Battalion, and Dorothea Elisabeth, nee Erb, of Friedewald, was born on 18 February 1777 between eleven and twelve o'clock noon in the winter quarters at New Brunswick, in the province of New Jersey, and baptized on 20 February 1777. Sponsor was

Coester Church Book

Catherina Elisabeth, wife of Grenadier Johann Henrich Iffert, of the Koehler Battalion.

David - son of Johann Reinhard Hence, grenadier of the von Linsing Grenadier Battalion, and his wife Margaretha, nee Eismann, of Hanau, was born during the morning of 19 February 1777 at Brunswick, and baptized 21 February 1777. Sponsor David Frise, grenadier of the von Linsing Battalion.

Maria Magdalena - legitimate daughter of Johann Paulus Schuck, sergeant in the Koehler Grenadier Battalion, and his wife Anna Christina Becker of Zierenberg, was born 20 February 1777 at New Brunswick, and baptized 23 February. Sponsor was Maria Magdalena, wife of Sergeant Metzer of the 2nd [English?] Guard Battalion.

Wilhelm Philipp - legitimate son of Grenadier Adam Koch, Sr., of the vacant Grenadier Company of the von Donop Regiment, from Oberbeisheim, District of Homberg, and his wife Maria Dorothea, of Hergetsfeld, District of Homberg, was born about four o'clock in the afternoon of 8 March 1777 at New Brunswick, and baptized the following day. Sponsor was Captain [Philipp Wilhelm] von Gall, present commander of the vacant Grenadier Company.

Dorothea Elisabeth - daughter of Grenadier Peter Stange of the von Lengercke Battalion, and his wife Catherina Elisabeth, first saw the light of day during our sea voyage from New York to Philadelphia, on 29 June 1777, and was baptized by me on 27 August. Sponsor was Dorothea Elisabeth, wife of Grenadier Johannes Gromann.

Johann Georg - legitimate son of Joseph Karl Wielteck, hunting horn player of the Ansbach Field Jaeger Company, and his wife Friederica Heinerica, was born on 13 November 1777 at Philadelphia, between eight and nine o'clock in the morning, and baptized in this city the following day, 14 November 1777. Sponsor was Johann Georg Bauer, field jaeger of Captain von Ewald's Company.

Coester Church Book

Johann Georg - legitimate son of Conrad Hase, grenadier of Captain von Gall's Company of the von Donop Regiment, and his wife Anna Elisabeth, was born on 27 November 1777 at Philadelphia, and baptized in this city on 29 November. Sponsor was Johann Georg Hase of the 2nd [English ?] Guard Battalion.

N.B. - Anna Elisabeth - legitimate daughter of Jacob Hartmann, musketeer in the Leib Company of the von Donop Regiment, and his wife Christina, nee Landau, of Lelbach, District of Hayna, saw the light of day in the camp at Philadelphia on 29 November 1777, and was baptized on 30 November. [Sponsor] was Anna Elisabeth, wife of Philipp Guembell, musketeer in the von Kutzleben Company of the von Donop Regiment.

Henrich Wilhelm - legitimate son of Christoph Humburg, field jaeger in the 1st Hessian Field Jaeger Company, and his wife Elisabeth Blum, born at Gudensberg, first saw the light of day in the camp at Philadelphia on 27 November 1777. I baptized him on the first day of Christmas month [1 December] 1777. His sponsor was Johann Henrich Gottfried Huene, field jaeger of the 1st Hessian Field jaeger Company.

Johann Friedrich - legitimate son of Peter Paul Wirth, field jaeger of the Hessian Field Jaeger Corps, and his wife Gerdruth, born at Nastaetten, District of Rheinfels, was born to the world at Philadelphia on 30 December 1777, at three o'clock in the afternoon. I baptized his on 5 January 1778. Sponsors were Johann Ewald, captain of the Jaeger Company, and Lieutenant Friedrich Adam Julius von Wangenheim, Hessian officer of the Jaeger Corps.

On 1 January 1778 I was again relieved by Staff Chaplain Heller, and returned to the von Donop Regiment.

Maria Magdalena - an illegitimate child, whose mother was Maria Magdalena Obersteig. Sponsor was Susanna Magdalena Aug, wife of a Philadelphia resident. She said Christian Krause, musketeer of the von Knyphausen Regiment, was the father.

Coester Church Book

N.B. - This person later married an Englishman.

Martha Elisabeth - the legitimate daughter of Recruit Nicolaus Barthel, born at Gernrode on the Eichsfelde, and his wife Anna Catharina Schwarzbach, from Erfurt (wedding certificate of Pastor Vilmann, 20 June 1777 at Kassel), was born on an English transport ship, on the voyage to America, on 21 March 1778, and baptized by me at Philadelphia on 10 May. Sponsor was Martha Elisabeth, wife of Corporal Reinhardi Roemer, of the Leib Company of the von Donop Regiment.

Johann Adam - was born on 22 November 1778 and baptized on 23 November 1778. Sponsor was Johann Adam Schmeck of Colonel von Gose's Company. The father was Joachim Kurz of Major von Kutzleben's Company, and the mother's name was Anna Catherina, nee Viemann, of Zimmersrode, District of Borken. This poor child was a complete abortion and had a growth like a turtle on his head. After conferring with Regimental Surgeon [Johann Jakob] Stieglitz, who considered it a human being, it was baptized in God's name. It died a quarter of an hour later. I was glad!

Baptisms in the Leib Regiment - Pastor Weidermann being sick.

Maria Catharina - born on 8 October 1778, baptized on 15 October 1778. The father was Jost Henrich Weising, of the Leib Company; the mother Gerdruth Helmrich, from Simmershausen, District of Kassel. Sponsor was Maria Catherina, wife of Sergeant [Samuel] Blum of Captain Waltenberg's Company.

Baptism in the Truembach Regiment

Bertold - born on 25 October 1778; baptized on 1 January 1779. Father Christian Scheele, musketeer in Colonel von Muenchhausen's Company; mother Elisabeth Bolt, from Hofgeismar; sponsor Berthold Koch of Captain Scheer's Company.

Coester Church Book

List of those Persons whom I Married during the Time I served as Chaplain of the von Donop Regiment

----

In Hesse

1. Adam Schuchard, sergeant in Lieutenant Colonel Heymell's Company, with Anna Martha Jacob from Homberg. Homberg, 14 February 1776.
   N.B. - This Sergeant Adam Schuchard cut his throat in the hospital at New York in 1782.
2. Reinhart Ludwig, musketeer in Major Hinte's Company, with Gertrutha Sophia Zelazin from [blank]. Homberg, 14 February 1776.
3. Adam Schmeck, drummer in Colonel von Gose's Company, with Anna Martha Volhars from Allendorf an der Ohm, Schweinberg District. Homberg, 14 February 1776.
4. Wilhelm Schroeder, musketeer in the Colonel's Company, with Anna Catherina Ritberg from Jesberg. Homberg, 14 February 1776.
5. Philipp Guembell, musketeer in Captain von Kutzleben's Company, with Anna Elisabeth Pflueger from Homberg. Homberg, 14 February 1776.
6. Paul Trischmann, musketeer in the Leib Company, with Catherina Schneider from Remsfeld, 14 February 1776.
7. Georg Schroeder, musketeer in Captain von Kutzleben's Company, with Anna Catherina Braun from Gumbeth. Homberg, 14 February 1776.
8. Johannes Hessler, musketeer in the Leib Company, with Anna Catherina Riel from Gumbeth on 21 February 1776.
9. Johannes Ide, musketeer in Lieutenant Colonel Heymell's Company, with Anna Elisabeth Weber from Waldesbrueck. Homberg, 28 February 1776.
10. Henrich Wolff, musketeer in Major Hinte's Company, with [blank]. Homberg, 28 February 1776/

Coester Church Book

11. Johannes Wahl, musketeer in Lieutenant Colonel Heymell's Company, with Anna Martha Scheuer from Reptich, District of Borken. Homberg, 28 February 1776.

12. Johannes Scheffer, musketeer in Colonel von Gose's Company, with Anna Elisabeth Hars from Roemersberg. Homberg, 28 February 1776.

13. Henrich Kehl, corporal in the Leib Company, with Maria Sabina Fuchs, daughter of Pastor Fuchs from Remsfeld. Homberg, 29 February 1776.

14. Conrad Riehl, musketeer in Lieutenant Colonel Heymell's Company, with Anna Martha Schanz from Udenborn. Homberg, 29 February 1776.

15. Henrich Wernert, grenadier in Captain Weitershausen's Company, with Anna Martha Rimmel from Verna. On the march to Heiligenrode, 2 March 1776.

16. Joachim Kurz, musketeer in Captain von Kutzleben's Company, with Anna Catherina Viemann from Zimmersrode, District of Borken. On the march to Uschlag in Hannover, 3 March 1776.

17. Johannes Haemer, musketeer in the Lieutenant Colonel's Company, with Maria Elisabeth Lohr from Freudenthal. On the march to Ronnebeck, District of Blumenthal, in Hannover, 17 March 1776.

18. Johannes Sustmann, musketeer of Colonel von Gose's Company, with Maria Elisabeth Wiederhold, daughter of the deceased Reinhard Wiederhold, born in Udenborn, District of Borken. Married in America on New York Island, in the camp at Bloomingdale, on 20 November 1776

(N.B.- Due to insufficient funds the groom could not pay the usual eight Reichsthalers. Colonel von Gose promised that it would be paid later.)

Leonora Luisa, the small daughter of Werner Dickhaut, musketeer in the von Donop Regiment, and Anna Gerdruth Pickhard, both born at Holzhausen, District of Homberg, was born at New York on 10 April 1777, and baptized on the thirteenth because I was present there. The sponsor was Leonora Luisa, wife of Corporal Toerfels of the Leib Company.

At this point is Jarock, runner for Colonel von Donop. He married a girl from Brunswick, in America, with the consent of his chief, at Kreton in the spring of 1777. The wife died at Brunswick on Long Island in December 1779.

(N.B. - This woman died at Bushwick in the fall of 1779)

On 3 August [1777] I married Johann Letzerich, non-commissioned officer of Captain Wach's 1st Company of the Hereditary Prince Regiment, and Martha Wacker, former wife of the killed-in-action Corporal Wacher, in the camp at Head of Elk.

On 15 September 1777, I married the Hessian Jaeger Conrad Sackert, of Major Prueschenck's Company, and Carolina Wetzler from Sebbeterode. This took place in the camp not far from Dellwerth in Pennsylvania.

N.B. - Major Prueschenck promised to collect the consent money and give it to me.

N.B. - Six days later the woman was chased out of camp for being a prostitute.

On 2 December 1777 I married Johann Burschel, grenadier from Captain Blesen's Company of the Guards Battalion and Sophia Meien, born at Kassel and widow of [the soldier] Meien, at Philadelphia

N.B. - [Missing]

On 19 November 1777 at Philadelphia, I married Grenadier Abraham Loehler, of the Lengercke Grenadier Battalion, and the young girl Elisabeth Well from Hesse-Hanau.

The first marriage which I performed
as a result of my duty with the von Lossberg Regiment
in the winter huts at Marsten's Wharf, 1778-1779.

After requesting permission of Colonel von Loos and the approval of Auditor Heymell, I married the following persons in the winter huts at Hellgate on 17 January 1779.

Coester Church Book

Fusileer Freidrich Busch, of the von Lossberg Regiment, born in Schermbach in Bueckeburg, 24 years old, and Wilhelmina Catharina, nee Ohm, widow of the dead Fusileer Ludwig Clausing of the mentioned von Lossberg Regiment. The groom was a foreigner and therefore did not have to pay the eight Thaler fee.

N.B. - The bride lost her husband only 21 weeks previously, therefore I could not marry her because of possible pregnancy, as cited in the law covering a year's mourning, but Captain [Major Ludwig August von] Hanstein and several other officers convinced me that the mentioned Wilhelmina Catherina, following the death of her previous husband - two weeks thereafter - had given birth, so because of the unavoidable circumstances of the war, I made no objections to the marriage.

Flushing on Long Island, 1 January 1779

After Carl Ludolph, grenadier of the von Lossberg Fusileer Regiment, born at Oldenburg, District of Schaumburg, received permission of his commander, Lieutenant Colonel [Wilhelm] von Loewenstein, to marry the widow Rosina Charlotta Leytmeier, also born in Oldenburg, and after paying the eight Reichsthaler and swearing an oath about his single status, the mentioned grenadier, after complying with the above requirements, was married on the above date to his bride without further objections.

N.B. - The widow, whose former husband had been killed during the siege of Charleston in April 1780, had not yet completed her year of mourning, but because his wife had not accompanied him [to South Carolina], there was no possibility of her being pregnant from her former husband.

New York, 13 January 1783, von Donop Regiment
Marriage

After Henrich Merten, soldier serving in Major von Kutzleben's Company of the von Donop Regiment, born at

Coester Church Book

Zwesten, District of Borken, received permission to marry, paid the eight Reichsthaler in cash for the maintenance of the Carlshaven Hospital for his first marriage, been approved by the auditor, and also been warned about swearing a false oath and sworn that he was single, I married him to his betrothed bride Anna Gerdruth Villgraff, nee Schick, born in Abteroda, District of Witzenhausen, widow of the dead Grenadier Erhard Villgraff, of the Linsing Grenadier Battalion, after being shown the death certificate.

N.B. - I gave each of them a marriage certificate at New York on 14 January 1783, as proof of the marriage.

Marriage

Upon receiving permission, as well as having taken an oath that he was single, and because there was no other objection, the soldier Michael Bernhard of the Leib Company of the von Donop Regiment, a foreigner born at Schwicks in Lothringen, was married by a priest to his betrothed bride, Charlotta de la Lime, daughter of Mr. Jean Baptiste La Lime, a resident of Quebec. This took place at New York on 2 February 1783.

N.B. - Both were Catholic.

Marriage

On 20 July 1783 I married, upon presentation of permission to marry from His Excellency, Commanding Lieutenant General [Friedrich Wilhelm] von Lossberg, Casimir Theodor Goerke, lieutenant of artillery, with the young lady, Elisabeth Roosevel [Roosevelt ?], born at New York.

Deaths

On 16 September 1781, at nine o'clock in the morning, Gemeling, the 66 year old sutler of the von Donop Regiment. I found by this man a firm belief, and his trust in God's grace was unfailing to the end. Fort Knyphausen.

On 5 January 1782 Conrad Giese, from Hundshausen in the Judicial District of Jesberg, died. During his final years, he was the cook for Colonel von Heymell, the commander of the von Donop Regiment. I was not told his age. His end was the easy

Coester Church Book

death of a Christian, who trusted his Redeemer to take him to a better world. He took communion twelve hours before his death.

Penance Situations in the von Donop Regiment

On 14 March 1776 I dismissed [the penance payment] of the following musketeers and their brides, namely: Georg Schroeder of Kutzleben's Company and his wife Anna Catherina Braun; and secondly, the Musketeer Johannes Hessler of the Leib Company and his wife Maria Catharina Riel, from Gumbeth.

Johann Adam Sustmann and his bride Maria Elisabeth Wiederhold stated their repentance to me on 20 November 1776, when I married them in America.

Johann Henrich Kramer, from Gilsa, District of Borken, was forgiven his penance payment on 24 December 1776 at New York, because of a situation with Anna Elisabeth Truemper of Reptig, District of Borken.

Penance Situations with the Donop Brigade at [New] Brunswick on 1 March 1777

1) From the Koehler Grenadier Battalion:
    a) From Captain Bode's Company
        Grenadier Johann Holzapfel - (I gave the certificate on 6 September 1783.)
        Grenadier Conrad Kilian - (I gave the certificate on 30 August 1783.)
        Grenadier Koch - (I gave the certificate on 6 September 1783.)
        Grenadier [Georg] Borck - (I gave the certificate on 30 August 1783.)
    b) Captain Hohenstein's Company
        Grenadier Georg Weber
        Grenadier Johann Jost Habbler

Coester Church Book

Grenadier Henrich Roese - (I gave the certificate on 1 November 1783.)

New Brunswick, 17 March 1777

[2.] From the von Minnigerode Grenadier Battalion

a) The non-commissioned officer Johann Georg Fehr, of the Vacant Hereditary Prince Company, born at Grebenau, District of Milsungen.

b) From Captain von Stein's Grenadier Company

Grenadier Christian Well, born at Treysa

Grenadier Conrad Spohr, from Linelbach, Judicial District of Doernberg.

At Easter, 30 March 1777

[3] From the Minnigerode Grenadier Battalion

Grenadier Justus Decker, of Captain von Stein's Company, from Arenborn, District of Feckerhagen

Grenadier Bernhard Schroeder, of Captain von Stein's Company, from [Gross] Ropperhausen, District of Ziegenhain

Grenadier Henrich Weber, Sr., from Stein, near Hattendorf, District of Neukirchen

Grenadier Christoph Thomas, of the Vacant Hereditary Prince Company, from Neuerode in the Judicial District of Pommeburg

At Philadelphia, on 28 February 1778, Musketeer Johannes Schroeder of Colonel Hinte's Company of the von Donop Regiment, born at Felsberg, came to see me and said that he had committed an act of fornication with Elisabeth Assemann from Felsberg. He was sorry to have committed the sin and promised to marry the unfortunate girl upon his return. As he then took communion, I dismissed payment of the penance.

Jamaica on Long Island

On 23 December 1780, Grenadier Christoph Blum (of von Gall's Company of the von Lengercke Battalion), from

Coester Church Book

Roemersberg, came to me and said that he had committed an act of fornication with Anna Catherina Wenderoth, born at Maisfeld, and the child, which was a girl, was still living. He promised to marry the woman.

Jamaica on Long Island

On 30 October 1780, the Artillery Sergeant Johann Henrich Brethauer, of the Leib Company, born at Klein Almarode, came to me and said that he had made an American girl, Polly Tiezen, from New York, pregnant and his child was still living. If he could be given permission, he would marry the woman, but in any case, would always support the child and mother.

At Jamaica on 30 October 1780

Johann Pflueger, of Captain von Gall's Company of the von Donop Regiment, from Wallenstein, District of Homberg, came to me and said he had committed an act of fornication with Catharina Elisabeth Aubel, from Falkenberg. According to later reports, the child was a son, born on Whitsuntide 1777 and died four weeks later.

N.B. - He promised to marry the woman.

At Flushing on 30 December 1780

Grenadier Burghard Zehr, of the von Knyphausen Regiment, born at Roelshausen, District of Neukirchen, declared that he had made a girl from New York pregnant, that he was truly sorry for his sin, and that to clear his conscience would like to have communion. As he swore on his oath to be more careful in the future and especially promised to conduct himself as a proper soldier, I allowed him to take communion with a clear conscience.

PS

Conrad Frey - the eldest son of Georg Adolf Frey, of Grossenkeder, and his wife Anna Margaretha from Vacha, was

Coester Church Book

born on 17 June 1778 on the English transport ship *Charming Nancy* during the voyage from Philadelphia to New York, and baptized in the camp at Marsten's Wharf, on Manhattan Island. Conrad Numme of Dommershausen, groom for Major General von Gose (the Colonel and Commandant of the von Donop Regiment), was the sponsor. I issued a baptismal certificate on 3 October 1783.

Coester Church Book

Register of Children Baptized in 1782

Anna Catherina - Daughter of Georg Haynlein, musketeer in the von Kutzleben Company of the von Donop Regiment, born in the Principality of Elbangen and in the city of the same name, and his wife Maria Catherina, nee Friderick, born at Caslaun in Zweibruecken, was legitimately born at Murray's house, not far from New York, at eight o'clock in the morning on 24 February 1782, and baptized on the 27th of the same month and year by me. The sponsor was Anna Catherina, nee Viemann, of Zimmersrode, wife of a musketeer of Major von Kutzleben's Company of the same regiment by the name of Joachim Kurz. (The baptismal certificate was sent to Nova Scotia on 6 September 1783.)

Prince Charles Regiment

Catherina Elisabeth - was born on the morning of 17 April 1782 on Manhattan Island about six English miles from New York City, and as her chaplain was unavailable, she was baptized by me on 19 April 1782. Johann Dietrich Pauly, born at Sontra, of the 4th [Company] and gunsmith of the Prince Charles Regiment, was the father. The mother was Elisabeth Haselbach, born at Rauschenberg. Catherina Elisabeth Sandmoeller, wife of the soldier [Friedrich] Sandmoeller of the Leib Company of the Prince Charles Regiment, born at Gilsa, District of Borken, was the sponsor.

Von Donop Regiment

Johann Valentin Engelhard - legitimate child, was born on 21 June 1782 in the camp near Fort Knyphausen, and baptized on the 23rd of the same month and year. The father was Christian Engelhard, soldier of the Leib Company of the von Donop Regiment, and the mother was Eva Barbara

Coester Church Book

Kahlstuetzer. Both parents were born in the same village, that is, Oberberges near Schmalkalden. A non-commissioned officer of the Young von Lossberg Regiment by the name of Johann Valentin Herdmann,, of the Leib Company, was the sponsor.

Miss Sarah Patterson - a lawful daughter of Mr. Stephen Patterson, assistant in the General Commissary Department in North America, and of his wedded wife Mrs. Sarah Patterson, was born on the 5th day of June 1782 and christened by my ministry on the 28th of June 1782. Mr. Tuck, lieutenant of the British Legion and Mrs. Falkener, both performing the duty of goships. The place where Miss Sarrah Patterson is born and baptized is called Harlem Valley, ten miles north of New York. I gave the certificate on 22 September 1782. *Mortus est.* [This entry is in English in the original. Gossip, not goship, is a no longer used form meaning godparent. The *"Mortus est"* is lined out in the original.]

Von Donop Regiment
Baptismal Certificate issued 15 May 1785

Bernhard Vogt - a legitimate son, was born during the night of 9 to 10 July 1782 in the camp near Fort Knyphausen, and baptized by me on the twelfth day of the same month and year. Jacob Vogt, a Catholic, born at Fritzlar and presently a soldier in the Leib Company of the von Donop Regiment, was the father and Christiana Sophia, born at Hannover Muenden, was the mother. Bernhard Naumann, soldier of the same company and born at Allmutshausen, District of Homberg, in Hesse, was the baptismal witness.

N.B. - Jacob Vogt, a very bad individual, much given to gambling and drinking, deserted from our service at New York in the year 1783.

Coester Church Book

Von Donop Regiment

Kilian Gassert - legitimate son, was born at New York on 29 January 1783, and baptized on 2 February 1783. Joseph Gassert, soldier in Colonel Heymell's Company of the von Donop Regiment, born at Wuerzburg and of the Catholic religion, was the father and his wife Eva Catherina, nee Linninger, from Aptey Everach, the mother. Kilian Klee, a soldier of the same company, from Zentersbach, in the Schwarzenfels (Zentersbach below Schluechternd) was the sponsor.

Von Donop Regiment

Catherina Elisabeth - (a legitimate daughter of the Musketeer Conrad Hirsch, of Major Kutzleben's Company of the von Donop Regiment, born at Odenheim in the Pfalz, and his wife Anna Margaretha, born at Stockstadt in Darmstadt) saw the light of day at New York on 23 February 1783, and was baptized by me on the 26th of the same month and year. In the name of his wife Catherina Elisabeth Ditmar, left behind in Hesse, Corporal Johann Wilhelm Ditmar of the same company, born in Hesse-Homberg, was the sponsor.

Prince Charles Regiment

Elisabeth - a legitimate daughter of the corporal by the name of Johannes Zerts, of Major General von Gose's Company of the Prince Charles Regiment, and his wife, nee Pflueger, born at Wickenrode, in the District of Kaufungen, was born in the Lisboner Brewery on the North River at New York on 3 March 1783, and baptized by me on the fifth of the same month and year. The godmother was the wife of Jost Eichlers, musketeer in Colonel von Lengercke's Company of the same regiment, Elisabeth Eichlers, born at Kreuzberg, District of Vacha (Philippsthal).

Coester Church Book
Artillery

Dorothea Elisabeth - a legitimate daughter of a cannoneer by the name of Wilhelm Scheffer, born at Kassel, and his wife Wilhelmina, nee Hanck, from Korbach, was born on 25 April 1783 at New York, and baptized on the first of May of the same year. Dorothea Elisabeth Eberhard, wife of Cannoneer Eberhard of the same company, was the godmother. (The mother was also a sponsor.)

Von Donop Regiment

Anna Catherina - legitimate daughter of the soldier (of Major von Kutzleben's Company of the von Donop Regiment) Joachim Kurz, and his wife Anna Catherina, nee Viemann, from Zimmersrode, was born at New York on 25 June 1783, at about two o'clock in the morning, and baptized on the 29th of the same month and year. Anna Catherina, wife of the soldier Georg Schroeder (Major von Wurmb's Company of the von Donop Regiment) gave the child its Christian name/

Artillery Regiment

Johannes Katzmann - the legitimate son of the Artillery Sergeant Johann Caspar Katzmann, of Captain Schleestein's Company, born at Brauenhausen, District of Rothenburg, and his wife Eva, nee Mayer, from Kassel, was born between nine and ten o'clock on 23 July 1783 at New York, and baptized by me on the 29th of the same month and year. His sponsor was a soldier of Captain Goebel's Company of the von Buenau Regiment by the name of Johannes Vogeler, born at Sontra, dd 2 Do. [This seems to indicate a fee of two dollars was paid.]

Young von Lossberg [Mirbach] Regiment

Anton Post - was born at New York on 9 August 1783, at ten o'clock in the evening and baptized on the thirteenth of the same month. Georg Post, from Breidenbach am Herzberge, Judicial District of Duerenberg (Doernberg/Hausen-Herzberg),

Coester Church Book

presently a soldier in the Leib Company of the Young von Lossberg Regiment, was the father and his wife Anna Kunigunde, of Heckelmanskirchen by Fulda, the mother. Anton Geise, musketeer of Major Baurmeister's Company of the same regiment, was the sponsor.

Young von Lossberg Regiment

Eva Catherina Sophia - was born to wedded parents at New York on 18 August 1783 and baptized on the 24th of the same month. Johann Friedrich Hartwig, born at Ersrode, District of Ludwigseck, Judicial District of Riedesel, was the father, and his wife Anna Catherina, born in New York - daughter of Johann Werner - was the mother. Johann Henrich Reichhard, a non-commissioned officer in the Prince Charles Regiment, held the child in the name of his sister, Eva Catherina Sophia Schultheiss, from Willingshausen, County Hersfeld, District of Niederaula, to be baptized.

N.B. - This Hartwig deserted shortly before our embarkation in America.

Artillery

Henriette Goerke - the legitimate daughter of the Hessian Field Artillery Lieutenant Casimir Theordor Goerke, and his lawful wife Mrs. Elizabeth Goerke, born at New York, was born near Fort Knyphausen - according to the father's statement - on 16 September 1783, and baptized at the same place by me on 16 October 1783. Mrs. Margaretha Cosine, wife of Mr. Cozine, a lawyer at New York, and the gentleman, Lieutenant Colonel Hans Henrich Eitel, commander of the Hessian Artillery in North America, were the solicited sponsors.

N.B. - Seven weeks and four days [later she died?].

Von Donop Regiment

Anna Catherina - the legitimate daughter of Drummer Adam Schmeck, of Colonel Heymell's Company, and his wife Anna

Coester Church Book

Martha, was born at New York on 15 October 1783, and baptized on the nineteenth of the same month. Sponsor - Reitze Amthauer, soldier of the same company, held the child for baptism in the name of his sister Anna Catherina, from Waltersbrueck. Died on the 21st of the same month, [and in Latin] may the ground rest lightly over her.

Martha Catharina - a legitimate daughter, was born in England at the royal barracks at Chatham, on 21 January 1784, to a grenadier of the von Ditfurth Regiment by the name of Jacob Dietrich, born at Viermuenden, and his wife Maria Margaretha, from Altenlotheim in Darmstadt, and baptized by me on the 25th of the same month and year, with Martha Catherina, [wife of a corporal] of the Prince Friedrich Regiment by the name of Conrad Pheil as sponsor. (Two dollar fee), date of the baptismal certificate 16 March 1783, Chatham.

Young von Lossberg Regiment

Anna Catharina - a legitimate daughter, was born to the sergeant major of Major Baurmeister's Company with the name Georg Henrich Reyers, and his wife Anna Maria, nee Sadler, from Harborn, during the night between 28 and 29 January 1784 at Chatham in England, and baptized on 2 February of the same year. Anna Catherina, wife of Corporal Hermann of the Leib Company of the Young von Lossberg Regiment, was the sponsor. (One-half gr[oschen], date of the baptismal certificate 16 March 1784, Chatham.

Von Donop Regiment

Andreas Maerten - a legitimate son, was born to wedded parents at Chatham in England on 15 February 1784. The father was a private soldier in the von Kutzleben Company of the von Donop Regiment by the name of Henrich Maerten, from Zwesten, District of Borken, and the mother's name was Anna Gerdruth, born at Ederode (Epterode ueber Witzenhausen),

Coester Church Book

District of Witzenhausen. On 17 February 1784 the child was presented for baptism in the name of Jesus by the honorable member of the von Donop Regiment (von Kutzleben Company) by the name of Andreas Carteuser, born at Wernswig, District of Homberg.

Artillery

Johann Caspar Freytag - legitimate son of the honorable artillery sergeant of the Schleestein Company by the name of Georg Freytag, from Kassel, and his wife Gerdruth, nee Kleinschmidt, from Melsungen, was born at Chatham in England on 19 February 1784, at four o'clock in the afternoon and baptized at the royal barracks at Chatham on the 22nd of the same month and year. Johann Caspar Katzmann, artillery servant, born at Brauenhausen, in the District of Rothenberg, was the solicited sponsor. (One-half gr., date of the baptismal certificate 16 March 1784, Chatham.)

Confirmations

On 20 October 1782, I confirmed Elisabeth Lentz - from Volmarshausen, a legitimate daughter of Johannes Lentz, private soldier in the D'Angelelli Regiment. According to the testimony, this Elisabeth was fifteen years old. She received a half-year of instruction on the Christian religion from me. I conducted this holy instruction in the Morris House, on the Island of York [Manhattan], in North America, in the presence of Major General von Gose and various officers of the Prince Charles Regiment. (Two dollars, certificate 21 January 1786.)

Friderica Rosina Jacobi - daughter of the dead Corporal Friedrich Ludwig Jacobi, who had been in Prussian service, was born on 17 May 1770 in Koenigsberg. Her mother Catherina Friderica, born at Ulm, was married to the soldier Christoph Stange, from Lochten, District of Finenberg, in the Heldesheim Monastery, of the von Donop Regiment. (Friderica Rosina was

Coester Church Book

confirmed by me, in the Christian religion, on 18 March 1784 at Chatham in England.

List of Baptized Children
Von Donop Regiment

Anna Catherina - legitimate child, born in the winter huts at Hellgate, on the Island of New York, on 5 January at four o'clock in the morning in the year 1779; baptized on 10 January 1779. Baptismal witnesses: Conrad Hassenpflug, grenadier in the 2nd Guards Battalion, and his wife Anna Catherina, born at Arolsen, capital of the Principality of Waldeck. Parents: 1) Father - Johann Galenus May, gunner with the von Lossberg [Artillery Detachment]. 2) Mother - Wilhelmina Leonora, born at Obernkirchen.

Von Lossberg Regiment

Sophia Wilhelmina - legitimate child, born on 21 January 1779 in the winter huts at Hellgate; baptized on 24 January. Parents: 1) Father - Johann Henrich Grages, corporal in Captain von Alten-Bakum's Company of the von Lossberg Regiment. 2) Mother - Dorothea Elisabeth, nee Moritz, born at Brake in Lippe. Sponsor: Sophia Wilhelmina, wife of Corporal Haak of the same fusilier regiment.

Wilhelm Justus - legitimate child, born on York Island in the winter huts at Hellgate on 2 January 1779, and baptized on the fifth of the same month. Parents: Johann Ernst Alhaus, sergeant in Colonel Scheffer's Company of the Lossberg Regiment. The mother's name is Anna Rebecca Sehrs, a Hanoverian from the District of Hoya. Baptismal witnesses: 1) Georg Wilhelm Helmerich, sergeant major of the above company. 2) Johann Justus Heidmueller, corporal of the same company.

Johann Henrich - legitimate child, born 10 April 1779 at Hellgate on New York Island, and baptized 11 April 1779. The

Coester Church Book

father, named Valentin Iffert, was quartermaster sergeant of the Leib Company of the von Lossberg Regiment. The mother was named Maria Catherina, nee Hencklein, from Bovenden. The sponsor was a field jaeger of Captain Wrede's Company by the name of Jost Henrich Iffert, (von Lossberg Regiment).

Baptized of the Graff Grenadier Battalion

Anna Catherina - legitimate child, born 27 February 1779, and baptized 4 March of the same year. Baptism and birth were on Staten Island. Father: Georg Thiel, grenadier in Captain Hessemueller's Company. Mother: Anna Maria Sehner, born at Hausen. Sponsor: Anna Catherina, nee Becker, from Zierenberg, the wife of Sergeant Schuck of the Hessemueller Company.

Anton - legitimate child, born 6 March 1779 on Staten Island, and baptized the following day. The father was Johann Henrich Hoffer, grenadier in Captain Hohenstein's Company. Mother - Catherina Elisabeth Steuber, born in Fridewald. Sponsor was named Anton Eichenauer, of Captain Neumann's Company.

Baptisms for other units

Ansbach Jaeger Corps

Friedrich Henrich - illegitimate child, born to Sally Thomson, daughter of Mr. Thomson, a resident of Philadelphia. The father supposedly is Captain Christoph Friedrich von Waldenfels, commander of the princely Ansbach Jaeger Corps. The infant was born to the world on 9 June 1779, not far from Kingsbridge in America, and baptized 5 July 1779. The sponsor was Captain Johann Friedrich Lorey, chief of a company of the illustrious Hessian Field Jaeger Corps. Baptism witnesses were Captain [Justus Friedrich] Venator of the von Donop Regiment and Lieutenant von Ebenauer of the Ansbach Field Jaeger Corps.

Coester Church Book

N.B. - The baptismal certificate was issued by the von Linsing Grenadier Battalion 25 August 1781.

Anna Dorothea - legitimate child, born to Elisabeth Roehrscheit, from Melsungen, presently the wife of Johann Daniel Ambrosius, non-commissioned officer in Captain von Mallet's Grenadier Company and wagonmaster of the von Linsing Grenadier Battalion. The infant saw the light of day on 3 July 1779, and was baptized on the fifth of the same month and year. Sponsor: Anna Dorothea, wife of Corporal Roehrscheit of Captain Wach's Grenadier Company. Not far from Kingsbridge in America.

Von Bose Regiment

Johann Christian Friedrich - legitimate child, born 23 July 1779 at Fort Knyphausen on New York Island, and baptized on 26 July of the same year. Father was a private soldier of Colonel von Bischhausen's Company of the von Bose Regiment, born at Lauben in Saxony and named Anton Weise. The mother was from Silessia and named Elisabeth, nee Dietrich. Sponsor was a sergeant from Colonel von Bischhausen's Company of the same regiment named Johann Christian Kersting, from Hombressen, District of Salsburg.

Von Lengercke Grenadier Battalion

Wilhelm Philipp - legitimate child, born 18 August 1779 in the camp on New York Island, and baptized the twentieth of the same month and year. Father called Dillmann Jacob von Zumpitz, born at Cologne and at the time grenadier in Captain von Gall's Company. Mother called Anna Rosina Scheurl, from Hirschfeld. Sponsor Captain von Gall, chief of the Grenadier Company of the von Donop Regiment.

Coester Church Book

Von Linsing Grenadier Battalion

Catherina Elisabeth - legitimate child, was born on York Island on 22 August 1779, and baptized on the 22nd of the same month and year. The father was a grenadier of Captain von Mallet's Company of the von Linsing Battalion by the name of Johannes Schuetz, from Rotenburg. The mother was Anna Maria Muenster, from Wippershain, [District of Hersfeld]. Sponsor Catherina Elisabeth, was the wife of Grenadier Roth of the von Linsing Battalion.

Von Bose Regiment

Anna Gerdruth - legitimate child, born 29 August 1779, on New York Island, and baptized 3 September of the same year. The father was Conrad Hund, born at Langenthal, District of Helmershausen, and a private soldier in Major DuPuy's Company of the Bose Regiment. The name of the mother was Martha Catherina, born at the same place. Sponsor Anna Gerdruth Flachshaar, from Hofgeismar, wife of Sergeant [Wilhelm] Flachshaar of the von Bose Regiment. The sergeant held the child in the name of his wife for the baptism.

Von Bose Regiment

Philippus - legitimate son, was born on New York Island on 10 September 1779, and baptized by me on the nineteenth of the same month and year. The father was Conrad Mohr, drummer in Major DuPuy's Company of the von Bose Regiment. The mother was Barbara Elisabeth, daughter of Gerhard Trinketrug, from Witzenhausen. Sponsor was Philipp Hunold, servant for Senior Surgeon Amelung and the son of the non-commissioned officer [Johannes] Hunold of the Prince Charles Regiment.

Von Donop Regiment

Conrad - legitimate son, was born on 23 September [1779 ?] on New York Island, and baptized the 26th of the same month and year. The father was a private soldier in Colonel Hinte's

Coester Church Book

Company of the von Donop Regiment by the name of Henrich Bierhenne. The mother was Anna Martha, nee Wiegandt, from Falkenberg, District of Homberg. Conrad Scheffer, non-commissioned officer of the same company was the sponsor. (Baptismal certificate issued 22 October 1783. The mother went with her second husband, Doenstaedt, a non-commissioned officer discharged by the von Donop Regiment, to Nova Scotia.)

Prince Charles Regiment

Johannes - legitimate child, born on New York Island in the Fort Laurel Hill on 16 October 1779, and baptized on the eighteenth of the same month and year. The father was Wilhelm Scheffer, born at Kassel, a cannoneer with the detachment with the Prince Charles Regiment, of Captain Schleestein's Company. The mother was Maria Wilhelmina Hancken, born at Korbach in the Principality of Waldeck. Sponsor Johannes Ostheim, born at Guntershausen, District of Kassel, was also a cannoneer of the same detachment and company.

Von Donop Regiment

Anna Catherina - legitimate child, born in winter quarters at Buckwick on Long Island on 22 November 1779, and baptized on the 28th of the same month and year. The father was the sergeant major of Colonel von Gose's Company, called Henrich Reinhard Roem. The mother was Martha Elisabeth Vanmueller, born at Homberg, in Hesse. Anna Catherina Ritberger, born in Jesberg, wife of Musketeer Wilhelm Schroeder of Major von Wurmb's Company, was the sponsor.

Hereditary Prince Regiment

Catherina Charlotta - an illegitimate child, was born at New York on 7 September 1779, and at the request of Lieutenant [Karl Friedrich] Fuehrer, baptized by me on 13 January 1780. The mother, a pleasant young girl, whose fate touched me, was named Cornelia, daughter of Mr. Bayeix, a citizen of New York.

Coester Church Book

She claimed the father was Lieutenant [Louis] Descourdes of the Hereditary Prince Regiment. He had caused her downfall with a promise of marriage - nothing new in America, unfortunately. (In 1783 the father took his discharge, married the girl, and went to Nova Scotia.)

Von Lossberg Regiment

Annette Luzie Margaretha - legitimate daughter, was born to Fusilier Georg Henrich Fock, of Colonel Schneider's Company of the von Lossberg Regiment, born at Guntersheim in the Earldom of Leiningen, and his wife Maria Catherina Leisner, born at Weinelsen, in the Pfalz, at Herricks on Long Island on 30 December 1779, and baptized by me there on 6 February 1780. The sponsor was Annette Luzie Margaretha, wife of Fusilier [Johannes] Trautwein, of the same company and regiment.

Andreas - an illegitimate son, was born at New York on 17 April 1780 to Barbara Rheider, born at Rhode Island and the daughter of the Anabaptist by the name of Rheider. The mentioned Barbara said Lieutenant Dietzel of the Hessian Artillery was the father, and that she had a child by him previously which was still living.

N.B. - She calls herself Mrs. Dietzel, because, she says, her marriage was made in Heaven. A soldier of the Leib Company of the von Donop Regiment, named Andreas Zuelch, was the sponsor on 20 April 1780 in New York. Therefore another pair of wretched boys and girls more in the world!

Therefore, take care and do not be fooled
By a man who promises to marry you!
(N.B. - Father and child died at New York in 1781.)

Von Buenau Regiment

Johanna Margaretha - was born on Staten Island on 3 May 1780, and baptized on the seventh of the same month and year. The father was a non-commissioned officer of the Leib Company

Coester Church Book

of the von Buenau Garrison Regiment, by the name of Franz Christoph Mangold, born at Eschwege. The mother was from the same place and named Anna Catherina, nee Gebhard. The two were legally married. Johanna Margaretha, the wife of Conrad Gross, cannoneer of the Leib Company of the Artillery Corps, was the sponsor.

Coester Church Book

1780

Elisabeth Christina - a daughter, was born to Georg Adolph Frey, born at Groszenkeder in the Schwarzenburg (servant to Major General von Gose), and his wife Anna Margaretha, nee Rosenthal, from Vacha, on 11 September 1780 at New York, and baptized on the fourteenth of the same month and year. The sponsor was Elisabeth Christina, nee Brand, wife of Fusilier Friedrich Huether, of the Hereditary Prince Regiment. (Died 18 September of the same year.)

Leib Regiment
Johann Valentin - the legitimate son of Cannoneer David Eberhard, from Kassel, of Captain Schleestein's Artillery Company, and his wife Dorothea Elisabeth Tippel, also born at Kassel, was born at New York on 19 September 1780, and baptized there on the 24th of the same month and year. The sponsor was Valentin Humburg, gunsmith of the Leib Regiment, also born at Kassel.

General Staff
Maria Elisabeth - Daughter of the Hessian provisions' administrator, by the name of Johannes Ebert, born at Wabern in the District of Homberg, and his wife Maria Elisabeth, nee Pelotrow, from New York, in America, was born at New York on 2 October 1780, and baptized by me at the request of both parents on the thirteenth of the same month and year. The mother herself acted as the sponsor and the baptismal witness was a good friend of theirs, by the name of Samuel Comphiel, a citizen and resident of New York.
N.B. - This Maria Elisabeth, wife of the provisions' administrator Ebert, was confirmed by me for a period of eight weeks in the Reform religion.

Coester Church Book

Von Linsing Grenadier Battalion
1780-1781

Johannes Franziscus - legitimate son of Grenadier Christoph Holzmueller, of Captain von Mallet's Company of the Linsing Grenadier Battalion, born at Bovenden, and his wife, Dorothea Ckaus, also of Bovenden, was born on 10 December 1780 in the camp at Jamaica on Long Island, and baptized by me on the twentieth of the same month and year. The sponsor was Johannes Franziscus Gottlob, grenadier of the same company, born at Wuerzburg.

N.B. - A Catholic.

Von Roeder Jaeger Company, Ansbach Service

Philipp Adam - legitimate son of Christian Conrad Rummel, field jaeger in Ansbach service, born in Ansbach, and in Captain von Roeder's Company, and his wife Margaretha Barbara Rincke, also born in Ansbach, was born at Flushing on Long Island on 18 January 1781, and baptized by me on the twentieth of the same month and year. The sponsor was Philipp Adam Wenig, private jaeger in Captain von Waldenfels's Company, also in Ansbach service.

Von Linsing Grenadier Battalion, 1781

Johannes, legitimate son of Grenadier Gerhard Fuellgraff, born at Epterode, District of Witzenhausen, and his wife Anna Gerdruth, nee Schick, of Epterode, was born on 11 February 1781 at Jamaica on Long Island, and baptized on the thirteenth of the same month and year. Sponsor, Johannes Schuetz, grenadier of the same company, was born at Rotenburg.

1781

Eva Elisabeth - was born on 17 March 1781 at Herricks on Long Island, and baptized on the 21st of the same month and year. She was the legitimate daughter of a mounted jaeger of

Coester Church Book

Lieutenant Colonel von Wurmb's Company, by the name of Caspar Schmid, born at Ulfen, District of Sontra, and his wife Anna Maria, nee Humburg, from Crumbach, District of Kassel. The sponsor was Eva Elisabeth, wife of the mounted jaeger Koerbel.

Von Donop Regiment, 1781

Maria Amalia - legitimate daughter of Hautboist Johann Ludwig Schmidt, of the von Donop Regiment, born at Fuhlen, in the District of Oldenburg, and his wife Maria Catherina, nee Brandenburg, from Hausbergen, not far from Prussian-Muenden, was born on York Island the afternoon of 13 April, and baptized on the fifteenth of the same month and year. Otto Friedrich Krueschel, sergeant major of Major von Wurmb's Company, was the sponsor in his wife Maria Amalia's name.

N.B. - The mother died on [blank] September 1781 of Slux [?]. The child was placed in a nursery at our cost because the father has nothing. (The child died 2 October 1781.).

Johannes - The legitimate son of Drummer Adam Schmeck, of the Vacant Colonel's Company of the von Donop Regiment, and his wife Anna Martha, was born on York Island on 18 May 1781, and baptized on the 23rd of the same month and year. Johannes Dickhaut, musketeer of the same company and regiment, was the sponsor. (Mgte) [?]

Jaeger Corps, 1781

Dorothea Christina - the legitimate daughter of Johann Christoph Wicks, field jaeger of Captain Ewald's Company, born at Kassel, and his wife Anna Maria, nee Losch, from Kassel, was born on Long Island on 15 June 1781, and baptized by me at Fort Knyphausen on 30 June 1781. Anna Dorothea, wife of Field Jaeger Friedrich Apt of the same company, was sponsor.

Coester Church Book

Von Donop Regiment

Johann Henrich - legitimate son of Joachim Kurz, musketeer (of Major von Kutzleben's Company) of the von Donop Regiment, and his wife, Anna Catherina, nee Viemann, of Zimmersrode, was born on 1 July 1781 at Fort Knyphausen, and baptized on the fifth of the same month and year. Sponsor was Musketeer Johann Henrich Schmidt of the same company.

Jaeger Corps Barracks at Fort Knyphausen (Prussian)

Johann Adam - legitimate son of Field Jaeger Michael Rupport, of Captain Ewald's Company, born at Aschaffenburg, and his wife Regina, nee Brand, from Worms, born 20 July 1781 on York Island, and baptized on the 23rd of the same month and year. Sponsor was the gunsmith of the Jaeger Corps, Johann Adam Pfaff. Catholic.

Jaeger Cor0ps, 1781

Johannes - legitimate son of Christian Lockberger, Hessian field jaeger in Captain von Donop's Company, born at Jena, and his wife Anna Catherina, nee Schreiber, from Seligenthal by Schmalkalden, was born at Fort Knyphausen on New York Island on 10 August 1781, and baptized on the fifteenth of the same month and year. His baptismal sponsor was Johannes Ulrich, musketeer in the Prince Charles Regiment.

Von Loewenstein Grenadier Battalion

Anna Catherina - was born in the camp at McGowan's Pass on New York Island on 22 August 1781 at four o'clock in the morning (so I am told), and baptized by me on the 23rd of the same month and year. The father was Nicolaus Boulanger, born at Marskirch in Lothringen, grenadier in the Ditfurth Grenadier Company (of Captain [Friedrich] Klingenden) of the von Loewenstein Battalion. The mother was Christina, nee May, of

Coester Church Book

Treysa in the District of Ziegenhain. The sponsor was Anna Catherina Mentzler, widow of the dead Grenadier Jacob Mentler, from Frankenberg.

Squadron

Daniel Heinbeck - was born on 1 September 1781 in the Jaeger camp at Kingsbridge on New York Island, and baptized by me on the sixth of the same month and year. The father was Johannes Stephan Heinbeck, private jaeger in the von Wurmb Squadron, born at Sohl in Electoral Saxony. Anna Catherina, nee Kaufhold, from Grossalmerode, was the mother. Corporal Daniel Selzam, of the von Wurmb Squadron, was the sponsor.

Artillery Detachment with the Jaeger Corps

Eva - daughter of Sergeant Gottfried Kip of Lieutenant Colonel Eitel's Artillery Company, born at Dittershausen in the District of Kassel-Neustadt, and his wife Martha Catharina, nee Vogeley, born in Allendorf, was born in the Jaeger camp at Kingsbridge on 7 September 1781, and baptized by me at that time. The sponsor was Eva, wife of the Artillery Servant Katzmann, of Captain Schleestein's Company, serving with the von Donop Regiment.

Jaeger Corps, 1781

Rosina - a legitimate child, was born on New York Island in the Jaeger camp below Fort Tryon on 17 September 1781. Her father, Peter Paul Wirths, private jaeger of Lieutenant Colonel von Prueschenck's Company, was born at Bonn, in Cologne. Gerdruth, nee Schunacher, from Nastaetten by Rheinfals, was the mother. The day of the holy rebirth of the newborn child was 19 September 1781, when Rosina, nee Ulrich, from Colmar, presently the wife of Corporal Seidling of Major von Wurmb's Jaeger Company, was the requested sponsor.

Coester Church Book

Squadron

Johanna Rosina Justina - a legitimate child, was born to the world on 26 September 1781 on York Island near the Morris House. Her father, Eusebrius Eremateich, born at Krumhendersdorf in Electoral Saxony, is presently a mounted jaeger in Lieutenant Colonel von Wurmb's Company. Anna Barbara, nee Ortwein, from Marburg, was the mother. The child was baptized on the 28th, when Rosina, nee Ulrich, from Colmar, wife of Corporal Seidling (of Major von Wurmb's Company) and the gunsmith for the Jaegers, Johann Adam Pfaff, were the requested sponsors.

Prince Charles Regiment

Johann Georg Frey - legitimate son of Georg Adolph Frey, born at Groszenkeder in the Schwarzenburg, presently servant of Major General Baron von Gose. The mother of the newly born was Margaretha, nee Rosenthal, from Vacha. According to the statement, the child was born on 6 October 1781, at four P.M., on York Island at the so-called Reed House. Upon request, I baptized it on 17 October 1781, with Johann Georg Wagner, servant of His Excellency, Lieutenant General von Knyphausen, as sponsor.

Von Donop Regiment

Anna Elisabeth - legitimate daughter of Johannes Scheffer, soldier in Colonel Heymell's Company, and his wife Anna Elisabeth, nee Hars, from Roemersburg, District of Borken, was born on 11 January 1782, at seven P.M. at Marsten's Wharf on York Island, and baptized on the fifteenth of the same month and year. Johannes Emloth, musketeer of Colonel Heymell's Company, born at Roemersburg, held the child to be baptized in the name of his sister, Anna Elisabeth Emloth.

Coester Church Book

Von Donop Regiment
Anna Elisabeth - a daughter, was born to Philipp Guembell of Major von Kutzleben's Company, and his wife Anna Elisabeth, nee Pflueger, from Homberg in Hesse, was born between five and six A.M., on 13 January 1782 on York Island, not far from Murphy's House, and baptized on the fifteenth. A soldier of the same company, named Conrad Opfer, of Hebel, District of Homberg, held the child for baptism in the name of the father's sister, Anna Elisabeth Guembell, from Oberurff-Schiffelborn.

Von Donop Regiment
Henrich Reinhard Dickhaut - legitimate son, was born on New York Island, not far from Marsten's Wharf on the East River, on 25 January 1782. His father was a musketeer in the Leib Company of the said regiment, named Werner Dickhaut, born at Holzhausen in the District of Homberg. The mother Anna Gerdruth, nee Pickhard, was also from Holzhausen. The newborn was baptized on the 29th of the same month and year. Sergeant-major Henrich Reinhard Roem, of Colonel Heymell's Company, was the sponsor.

[Artillery] Detachment with the Prince Charles Regiment
Elisabeth Scheffer - a legitimate child, was born on 8 February 1782, about five P.M., at McGowan's Pass on York Island, and on the tenth of the same month and year, baptized by me upon request. Wilhelm Scheffer, born at Kassel, cannoneer in Captain Schleestein's Company, was the father, and his wife Maria Wilhelmina, nee Hanck, of Korbach in the Principality of Waldeck, was the mother. Elisabeth, wife of the soldier Eichler, of Colonel von Lengercke's Company of the Prince Charles Regiment, was the sponsor.
    N.B. - The sponsor was from Philippsthal, District of Vacha.

Coester Church Book

Von Donop Regiment

Anna Catharina - a legitimate daughter, was born to the world on 12 February 1782 near the city of New York and on the seventeenth of the same month and year, baptized by me. Christoph Stange, from Lochtum, District of Vienenburg, Monastery Hildesheim, presently musketeer in Major von Wurmb's Company of the von Donop Regiment, was the father. Catherina Friederica, born in Ulm, was the mother. Anna Catherina, wife of Musketeer Georg Schroeder, of the same company, was the sponsor. (dd baptismal certificate in March 1784.)

Names of Those I have Confirmed in my Role as Chaplain

On Easter, 31 March 1777, I confirmed two lads, who had already been taken on by the von Minnigerode Battalion as fifers. Both were children with good spirits and healthy intellects. I had instructed them in religion for nine weeks and never worked with greater pleasure than with these children. I easily gave them the basis for our religion, allowed them to memorize some - and how supple the human heart can be, when a person has found the right way! They learned the words of consolation from the Bible and also the first five chief articles without being forced to do so by me. It is good for you", I often said, "my children. It will give you courage in danger and consolation in death, if you also keep it in mind." That is what I said and those few words were enough to impress their tender souls. They gave me great pleasure here. How great it will be in the hereafter. May my future students give me the joy which these first ones gave me! The older was Johannes Krueck, born at Rinteln in 1763. His father was a grenadier in Captain von Wilmowsky's Company, named Henrich Krueck. The other [nothing more follows]

Coester Church Book

On 19 May 1780 I confirmed a young girl, thirteen years old, at New York, in the presence of her parents. Her name was Anna Elisabeth Gleim, born at Melsungen on the Fulda. The father was Johannes Gleim, born at Hersfeld and a fifer in Captain von Mallet's Grenadier Company, of the von Mirbach Regiment. The mother, Elisabeth, nee Pflueger, was born at Rotenburg.

N.B. - This girl gave me much pleasure, not only because of her eagerness to learn, but also, because of her outward decorum, not a little joy.

Martha Elisabeth Schaeffer - from Harle, District of Flensberg, who was confirmed by Chaplain Kuemmell at Rhode Island in 1778, because she could show no confirmation testimonial, was privately examined, and based on the remarks of her then master, the master baker Ostwald, of New York, she was admitted to the sacrament. Certificate issued 12 May 1780.

N.B. - The parents are father: Henrich Schaefer, sergeant in the von Huyn Regiment; mother: Anna Elisabeth, nee Ditmar, from Singlis, District of Borken.

Comment - Chaplain Kuemmell was at Charleston with the von Huyn Regiment at that time.

On the second Easter Day, that is 1 April 1782, I confirmed Friedrich Almeroth, born at Homberg in Hesse in March 1768, after he gained the proper knowledge of the Christian religion, following his having reached his fourteenth year, in an open assembly at Marsten's Wharf, on the Island of New York. The father was the Captain-at-arms of the Leib Company of the von Donop Regiment, by the name of Georg Almeroth. The mother was Egidia Almeroth, born at Hersfeld.

Coester Church Book

Supplement

On 9 September 1776 I was asked by a friend to baptize the five year old child of an inhabitant on Long Island, because the pastor had joined the rebels. I made some objections because I had not acquired sufficient proficiency in the English language to make myself understood to the people. However, the persistent entreaties of the parents overcame my objections. I was there and baptized the child according to our practice, with the regimental surgeon in attendance. The child was a girl. The sponsor was named Elisabeth Plaaumens, and named it Merry [Mary ?].

The father was a poor shoemaker named Thomas Pauer; the mother Isabella Pauer. The place where they lived was a pleasant and lively little village directly opposite New York, by the name of Brooklyn Ferry. Father and mother wept for joy over their good fortune that now their beloved child had been taken into the Christian fold by the bond of baptism. They spoke continual praises for me. And, as they had nothing else with which to show their appreciation, I had to drink a half glass of wine with the woman who had just had a delivery.

Long Island, in the camp at Brooklyn Ferry, 9 September 1776 (Cannon Beach)

Members of the von Donop Regiment of re-enactors
(photograph by Bruce Burgoyne.)

Journal
of the
Hesse-Cassel
Von Donop Regiment

**Maintained by
Regimental Quartermaster**
Johann Georg Zinn

Donop Regimental Journal

Johann Georg Zinn

Johann Georg Zinn, born in 1743, was the regimental quartermaster of the Hesse-Cassel von Donop Regiment. As such, it was his duty to maintain the regimental journal. Very little seems to be known about Zinn, other than what he recorded in the journal. From the journal it can be seen that he sailed to America with the regiment in 1776, served throughout the war as the regimental quartermaster, and returned to Europe with the regiment in 1784. His journal entries are few and brief with no explanation for the paucity of entries. As with most of the Hessians, who wrote the various documents concerning the American Revolution, their written observations provide the only knowledge of the men and once back in Germany, the authors fade from the pages of history.

Donop Regimental Journal

Introduction

The following journal of the von Donop Regiment is the shortest regimental journal I have encountered. The von Mirbach Regimental Journal and the Platte Grenadier Battalion Journal are both much more detailed. Possibly the von Donop Journal is so brief because the regiment saw only limited combat service after 1776. Even the capture of Fort Washington is covered in the journal with only a few sentences, and here, too, the regimental combat role was of minor importance.

However, the journal provides lists of the unit officers and names of the ships on which the regiment sailed. And, as noted earlier, the journal is useful for helping to identify the author, von Bardeleben, of the anonymous diary, and confirming entries in other documents.

Donop Regimental Journal

Journal of the Illustrious
von Donop Regiment
(later) the von Knyphausen Regiment
From 29 February 1776, the day of marching out of Hesse
to 17 May 1784, the
day of marching back
into garrison at Kassel.
Maintained by the Auditor and Regimental Quartermaster
[Johann Georg] Zinn

- - - - - - -

On 29 January 1776, in accordance with orders received, the illustrious von Donop Regiment marched out of its previous quarters in the city of Homberg, at seven o'clock in the morning, and began the trip to America.

The mentioned regiment, including the Grenadier Company, which, together with three other grenadier companies, had previously been detached to form the von Block Grenadier Battalion, consisted of six companies and in each were the following officers

I - Grenadier Company
Captain [Friedrich Karl] von Weitershausen, commanding
1st Lieutenant [Friedrick Wilhelm] Geisler
2nd Lieutenant [Johann Philipp] Reiss
2nd Lieutenant [Karl August] Freyenhagen, Sr.

II - Leib [Body] Company
Lieutenant General [Wilhelm Henrich] von Donop, who was ordered to remain behind in Hesse (commander of the Kassel garrison)
Captain [Philipp Wilhelm] von Gall
2nd Lieutenant [Emanuel Rosinus] Hausmann
Ensign [Wilhelm Johann Ernst] Freyenhagen, Jr.

Donop Regimental Journal

III - Colonel's Company
Colonel [David Ephraim[von Gose, acting regimental commander
Captain [Christoph Dietrich] von Donop
2nd Lieutenant [Karl Friedrich] von Nagel, Sr.
Ensign [Franz Karl] von Staedel

IV - Lieutenant Colonel's Company
Lieutenant Colonel [Karl Philipp] von Heymell
Captain [Johann Matthias] Gissot
2nd Lieutenant [Johann Heinrich] von Bardeleben
Ensign [Eitel Wilhelm] von Trott

V - Major's Company
Major [Erasmus Ernst] Hinte
1st Lieutenant [Justus Friedrich] Venator
2nd Lieutenant [Henrich Ludwig] von Nagel, Jr.
Ensign [Karl] von Knoblauch

Middle Staff
Adjutant - Lieutenant [Wilhelm Karl] von Donop
Regimental Quartermaster - [Johann Georg] Zinn
Auditor - [Bartholomai Ernst] Heymell
Chaplain - [Georg Christian] Coester
Regimental Surgeon - [Johann Jakob] Stieglitz

The regiment marched to Doernhagen, Albshausen, and Coerle, where it had quarters the first night, and was assigned as follows: the staff, the Colonel's and the Major's Companies at Doernhagen; the Lieutenant Colonel's and Captain von Kutzleben's Companies at Coerle; and the Leib Company at Wolleroda and Albshausen.

1 March - We, the staff, and the Colonel's and Major's Companies went to Heiligenroda; and

Donop Regimental Journal

The Leib, Lieutenant Colonel's, and von Kutzleben Companies to Nieder Kauffung, into night quarters.

2 March - A day of rest.

3 March - We marched to Uschlag and Benderoda. The staff, Colonel's and Major's Companies took night quarters in the former; and the Leib and Lieutenant Colonel's Companies in the latter place.

4 March - We marched to Mengershausen, where the staff, Colonel's, Major's, and von Kutzleben Companies received quarters. The Leib and Lieutenant Colonel's Companies however, went to Vockeroda.

5 March - The staff, Colonel's, and Major's Companies received quarters in Ostheim, County Brunstein; the Leib and Lieutenant Colonel's Companies went to Hollenstaedt, County Salzderheiden; von Kutzleben Company in Stockern, County Rothen Kirchen.

6 March - The regiment had a day of rest at the mentioned locations.

7 March - We marched and the staff, Leib, Colonel's, and Major's Companies received night quarters in Dillesen; the Lieutenant Colonel's and von Kutzleben Companies in Keyer. From here we marched on

8 March - to Geestendorf, where the staff and the entire regiment were quartered.

9 March - The night quarters for the staff, Leib, Colonel's, and Major's Companies was in Kohlefeldt. The Lieutenant Colonel's and von Kutzleben Companies however, went to Lueden.

10 March - There was a day of rest here.

11 March - We marched to Hoemsen, where the staff and Colonel's and Major's Companies entered quarters, then to Gottesbuendel, where the Lieutenant Colonel's and von Kutzleben Companies stayed, and the Leib Company went to Rohsen.

Donop Regimental Journal

12 March - The staff, Colonel's and Major's Companies lay at Hoershagen, von Kutzleben's Company at Duetenhausen, the Lieutenant Colonel's Company at Dedendorf, and the Leib company at Dittershausen.

13 March - Quite unexpectedly, as we were about to march during the morning, a day of rest was ordered, and we remained here until

14 March - when we marched to Kirch- and Suedeweihe. The staff, Colonel's, Major's, and Kutzleben Companies entered quarters in the first, and the Lieutenant Colonel's and Leib Companies the latter place.

15 March - The staff, Colonel's, and Major's Companies marched to Verbungdam, von Kutzleben's Company to Rosom, and the Lieutenant Colonel's and Leib Companies to Steindorf, where the assigned quarters were occupied.

16 March - The designated quarters were entered, with the staff and Major Hinte's Company in Blumenthal; the Leib Company at Omont and Schren, Colonel von Gose's Company in Beckendorff, the Lieutenant Colonel's Company in Vegesack, and Captain von Kutzleben's Company in Ronnebeck and Fargo, where until

17 March - we remained and had a day of rest, but on the following day,

18 March - we resumed our march and the staff, Colonel's, and Major's Companies received quarters in Haagen; the Leib company in Druefftele; Lieutenant Colonel Heymell's Company in Dorfhaagen; and Captain von Kutzleben's Company in Raseburg.

19 March - The staff and Major Hinte's Company moved into cantonment quarter in Stadel; the Leib Company in Nesse; the Colonel's Company in Losten and Lahnhausen; and the Lieutenant Colonel's and von Kutzleben Companies in Lechstaedt, where we remained lying until 3 April, when the regiment moved out and marched to Ollsdorff, not far from Bremerlehe, where we were mustered in the presence of Colonel

Donop Regimental Journal

[William] Faucitt and administered the oath. We then marched back into the former quarters.

9 April - The regiment was embarked at Bremerlehe on the following ships: *Esche, Empress, Jenny,* and *Hope*, and remained lying at anchor in the Weser until

16 April - when all the ships, under the supervision of Agent Parker, entered the sea for England and were underway until

20 April - After entering the [English] Channel this night we lay at anchor. Toward six o'clock this morning, we again raised anchor. At nine-thirty we arrived at Spithead, not far from Portsmouth, and dropped anchor there.

29 April - The regiment had only four ships from Bremerlehe here, and such were too crowded. We received a fifth one here, named *Surprise*. Therefore officers as well as soldiers were transferred from other ships.

First, from *Hope*, Captain Venator and 34 men of von Kutzleben's Company.

Second, from *Esche*, Lieutenant von Nagel, Sr., and Lieutenant von Nagel, Jr., and 34 men from von Kutzleben's Company.

Third, from *Jenny*, Ensign Knoblauch and 33 men.

Fourth, from *Empress*, thirty men of the Leib Company, so that the command on the ship *Surprise* consisted of one captain, three officers, and 131 men.

3 May - Today we received provisions for the regiment from Portsmouth.

4 May - At six o'clock this morning we raised anchor and sailed to the Isle of Wight, where we again anchored nearby at seven-thirty.

6 May - At six o'clock this morning we went underway. Our fleet was 44 sail strong, with forty English [ships], making a total of 84 transport ships. Our escort consisted of six warships and Commodore [William] Hotham was in command.

Donop Regimental Journal

10 May - Today we left the Channel and entered the ocean. The commodore raised his flag on the warship *Preston*, 52 cannons, and therefore was saluted by the other warships firing their cannons, which compliment, he also acknowledged from his ship.

18 May - Toward eight o'clock this evening the ship *Speedwell*, on which Colonel [Justus Henrich] Block was assigned, passed near us. His ship had developed a leak and had to employ four pumps constantly to remove the water.

21 May - Toward twelve o'clock the wind became very strong, so that our after-mizzenmast broke.

30 May - After the stormy weather, which had continued uninterrupted for nearly seven days, abated somewhat, the commodore raised the signal this morning for all ships' captains to report on board his ship to received a sealed order giving the place of rendezvous in case they became separated from the fleet.

4 June - On this day, the King's birthday was celebrated by all the warships firing their cannons at one-thirty.

22 June - Today we passed the middle-most Grand Bank near Newfoundland. The thick fog, which had persisted for several days, had caused the fleet to become widely scattered, so that on

23 June - the commodore gave a signal to wait for the ships which had fallen behind.

24 June - About two o'clock this morning Ensign von Staedel, who had lain sick with an inflammatory fever already for some time, died on board the ship *Esche*, and this same evening at eight-thirty was buried overboard, in the water.

26 June - Our ship and four others had become separated from the fleet in the thick fog and we sailed alone until about one o'clock in the afternoon, when we received an order from a frigate that we were to wait for a bomb galley with nine ships, which were some miles behind us, so that we could then continue on our way with thirteen ships.

Donop Regimental Journal

3 July - Toward evening the fog cleared and we saw the coast of Nova Scotia.

4 July - About ten o'clock in the evening we anchored not far from the harbor at Halifax.

5 July - At four o'clock this morning we raised anchor and arrived in the harbor at Halifax at twelve o'clock noon, with eleven transport ships, one bomb galley, and one frigate, and dropped anchor again.

6 July - All the ships' captains had to report on board the bomb galley, where they were informed that Sandy Hook was the rendezvous, and at six-fifteen we again left the local harbor and entered the ocean.

7 July - About eight o'clock this morning we again met and joined the main fleet. At two o'clock in the afternoon the commodore made a signal for all the ships' captains and again ordered that Sandy Hook was to be the rendezvous, and we continued to sail onward.

6 August - Our ship's captain took a sounding today and found bottom.

11 August - About three o'clock in the afternoon we again saw land for the first time to our right, and it was the coast of Long Island.

12 August - About four o'clock this afternoon we anchored near Sandy Hook, where some of the ships, which had remained behind for the Mirbach, Rall, and von Knyphausen Regiments, sailed past, and rejoined our fleet.

15 August - All the regiments of the 1st Division landed and entered camp on Staten Island, where on

16 August - they were provided with fresh and salted provisions.

21 August - Colonel von Donop's Brigade, consisting of the Jaegers and three grenadier battalions, was embarked on flat boats and on

22 August - sailed to Long Island, where they landed without meeting any resistance.

Donop Regimental Journal

26 August - Our regiment broke camp on Staten Island and sailed in flat boats to Long Island, where we entered camp not far from Flatbush.

27 August - The enemy was attacked by the English at daybreak/ The von Donop Regiment was in camp just below the hill which the grenadiers marched up in order to attack the enemy. The regiment had to move out at about ten o'clock in the morning to occupy the woods behind the grenadiers. The regiment made no direct contact with the enemy, but several patrols sent out, captured 83 rebels, including eight officers. We remained under arms, near these woods during the night and until the morning of

28 August - when we again entered our former camp. This did not last long, however, because at one o'clock in the afternoon the regiment again broke camp, and marched through Flatbush to a height on the other side of the woods, where we entered camp within sight of the enemy defenses.

30 August - After the enemy left his besieged camp during the previous night and crossed over the East River to New York Island, we again broke camp at one o'clock noon and marched into the enemy line. Since then the von Donop Regiment has been divided into four parts to occupy the various defenses. The regimental baggage remained at Brooklyn, a village, under the open sky and we bivouacked until

15 September - At two-thirty in the morning the regiment broke camp, leaving knapsacks and tents, as well as the regimental artillery behind, and marched farther up the East River, where it then was carried across the river at four o'clock in the afternoon with the Hereditary Prince and Mirbach Regiments, as the three regiments now constituted the brigade of Major General [Johann Daniel] Stirn, landed in the region called Turtle Bay, and occupied a height not far from the bay, where it bivouacked this night until

Donop Regimental Journal

16 September - when we entered the campsite designated for the regiment near Bayard's House on the North river. We remained undisturbed in this camp until

1 October - when we moved forward about two miles and entered the camp near Mr. John's house.

16 November - Fort Washington was attacked from the opposite side of Kingsbridge. The von Donop Regiment had to move forward another two miles, but did not come under fire, but Lieutenant von Nagel, Sr., with thirty men and Lieutenant von Lepel, with fifty men were detached. The first drove the enemy from his defenses, which contained a cannon; from the second detachment, two men were wounded.

After the fort was captured, the regiment moved back into camp toward evening, where the regiment remained until

5 December - when we entered winter quarters in New York and were assigned five individual houses in Queen Street and Hannover Square and Water Street. During our stay in these winter quarters, nothing of consequence occurred in the regiment. In addition to our regiment, the garrison consisted of the Hereditary Prince and Mirbach Regiments and several English regiments.

27 December - The confirmed report was received that Colonel Rall's Brigade had been attacked at Trenton and made prisoners of war.

Donop Regimental Journal

[1777 -- And the rest of the War]

After having spent our time quite peacefully in our winter quarters in New York, we received, on

3 July [sic - June] - an order of today's date, to be prepared to embark and the von Donop Regiment, on

5 June - at five o'clock in the morning, was embarked on three transport ships on the North River.

1) *Charming Nancy* - Colonel von Gose, Captain von Donop, both Lieutenants von Nagel, Lieutenant von Lepel, Ensign Freyenhagen, the regimental surgeon, Artillery Lieutenant Kayser, and 285 non-commissioned officers and men.

2) *Hope* - Colonel Heymell, Major Hinte, Captain Gissot, Lieutenants Reiss and von Lossberg, Ensign von Trott, Auditor Heymell, and 191 men.

3) *Neptune* - Captain Venator, Lieutenant Murhard, Lieutenant Hausmann, Ensigns von Knoblauch and Murhard, the regimental quartermaster, and 159 men.

In addition to our regiment, the Leib and Mirbach Regiments, which three regiments made the brigade of Major General Stirn, and several English regiments, were also embarked, so that our corps consisted of approximately 4,000 men.

7 June - We set sail about ten o'clock in the morning, passed the so-called Narrows, between Staten and Long Island, and then anchored in Raritan Bay. We lay there until

8 June - At eight o'clock we raised anchor and sailed to Port Amboy, where we arrived at twelve-thirty, landed, and entered camp near this small city. We remained there until

12 June - when at daybreak the entire army moved out and marched to Brunswick, where we arrived at about twelve o'clock noon, and entered camp in a small city called Landingen, on the other side of the Raritan River. The English headquarters of General [William] Howe was at Brunswick.

Donop Regimental Journal

13 June - At about nine o'clock in the evening we received march orders, and the tents were immediately taken down, the wagons packed, and the army stood under arms until

14 June - At two o'clock in the morning we crossed the bridge over the Raritan outside Brunswick, and on the same day marched onward to Middlebush. All the tents and baggage remained in Brunswick, where houses were assigned for our use. We remained near Middlebush, always in bivouac, until

19 June - when, at daybreak, we marched back to Landingen, crossed the bridge, and entered the camp on the other side at the Raritan River. We moved out of this camp on

22 June - at daybreak, and marched back to Amboy. During our march the enemy attacked our rearguard with great success. As soon as we arrived at Amboy, we were taken across to Staten Island in flatboats, and marched onward to Princess Bay. Because our tents and baggage could no longer be sent across this evening, we had to bivouac.

23 June - Our tents and baggage arrived toward morning and the camp was set up.

24 June - At nine o'clock in the morning we again received orders to take down our tents and to embark on board the previously listed ships, which were lying in the bay, not far from the camp. Today Lieutenant General [Leopold] von Heister took his departure from command of the army. This embarkation took place with the intention of returning to Amboy, to drive back the ever-continuing pressure from the enemy.

26 June - We again received orders to debark. We were to have sailed to Amboy with the troops on the transport ships, but the light winds and the ebb tide, which just at that time ran against the ships, prevented it, and the debarkation could not take place until

27 June - at two o'clock in the morning, and even then, the troops on the *Charming Nancy*, which had run aground on a sandbank, had to travel nearly three English miles, or one

Donop Regimental Journal

[German] hour, in flatboats, to the landing place at Amboy. At that place the brigade of General von Stirn was formed, and because the cannons or the von Donop Regiment could not be brought up so quickly, it was necessary to take the artillery of the Koehler Battalion until, after several hours, their own regimental guns arrived. The von Donop Regiment and the Combined Battalion and an English regiment remained near Bonhamtown, in order to cover the army's left flank from a height. After the enemy, according to plan, had been driven back, the regiment marched back to Amboy at one o'clock, where it also, because the other regiments were with the main corps and had already returned, embarked alone. The heat was so exceptionally great on this day that several soldiers collapsed and died on the march.

28 June - The army returned and was transferred across to Staten Island in boats, and all the transport ships lying at anchor at Amboy sailed, after Amboy had been evacuated by the British, back to Princess Bay, where even more transport ships lay, in order to take the rest of the troops [on board]. Then, after all the troops had been embarked, and a part sent to New York, the ships sought better anchorage inside The Narrows, near Cole's Ferry, and awaited additional sailing orders. Therefore, finally on

19 July - a signal to raise anchor was made with a cannon shot from the admiral's ship, called the *Eagle*, on which was Admiral [Richard, Lord] Howe, who commanded the fleet, but it remained in the area until

20 July - at nine o'clock in the morning, when a signal to set sail was again made. We actually got under way, but once again had to drop anchor in the bay at five o'clock in the afternoon, because of contrary winds and a strong flood tide. We lay here until

21 July - at six o'clock in the morning, when we made another attempt [to sail], but had to anchor again at nine-thirty. Finally, at twelve o'clock noon, a favorable wind arose with

Donop Regimental Journal

which we sailed to Sandy Hook and lay at anchor there with the other ships.

23 July - At eight o'clock this morning a signal was made to raise anchor and all the ships of the fleet crossed the bar in the bay and entered the ocean with a rather favorable, but weak, wind.

30 July - At seven-thirty this morning we saw Maryland, and sailed past the mouth of the Delaware [Bay], finally entering Chesapeake Bay, and later entered the Elk River, where, on

25 August - we debarked and entered the camp near Elk Ferry.

31 August - Today we marched to Elk Ferry, where we were shipped across the Elk River in flatboats, and landed near Sicily Court House. From that place we went onward to Sicily Church, where we made camp.

2 September - We marched to Garrison's Tavern and made camp there. We remained until

3 September - then marched to Aiken's Tavern. From there we had to send all heavy baggage and the tents back to the ships, and had to make huts from bushes.

8 September - We marched to a place whose name is still unknown to us, and camped not far from it.

9 September - At three o'clock this afternoon we broke camp and marched until six o'clock the following day.

10 September - Then we entered camp at Connart's Tavern and built huts.

11 September - We broke camp at four o'clock this morning and the battle at Brandywine Hill began. After the battle, the regiment and several English regiments were ordered onto a height to cover the baggage, where we remained until three o'clock in the middle of the night on

12 September - and then marched to Dilworth and entered a camp of huts, where we remained quietly until

Donop Regimental Journal

16 September - At five o'clock in the morning we broke camp and marched until eight o'clock in the evening, when we built a camp of huts and remained lying there until

18 September - We marched at daybreak and again entered camp near Valley [?].

21 September - We left the camp at daybreak and marched to Charlestown, where we entered camp.

23 September - At moonrise we moved out from here again, and after we had waded through the small Schuykill River, we again built huts and remained therein until

25 September - when we continued our march and entered camp not far from Germantown. In this camp we were again rather peaceful until

4 October - when at daybreak we were alerted and the enemy suddenly attacked, which developed into a general battle and engagement between the two armies, but in which the regiment did not participate. Nevertheless, General von Stirn., in whose brigade the regiment served, received a bruise from a small ball.

19 October - We marched from here back to Philadelphia, where we set up camp, behind the line, not far from the city.

4 December - We marched out of this camp at nine o'clock in the evening on an expedition to Chestnut Hill. The camp was left standing.

5 December - We arrived at Chestnut Hill at daybreak. In addition to the English engaging the enemy here, nothing of further consequence occurred.

6 December - At nine o'clock in the evening we marched from here to Edgehill and arrived there on

7 December - at daybreak. We remained here until

8 December - at one o'clock noon, and then marched on to the former camp near Philadelphia, which we entered at seven o'clock in the evening. We remained undisturbed in this camp until

Donop Regimental Journal

30 December - when the regiment marched into winter quarters in Philadelphia, and was quartered in the lower part of Philadelphia, in various houses and streets.

20 May 1778 - When the news arrived that the enemy was moving the captives of General Burgoyne's army to Virginia, and that they were already underway, in the near vicinity, the entire garrison, including our regiment, received marching orders. We marched to Germantown and occupied that region in the hope of attacking the enemy. However, on the same day, we marched back to Philadelphia.

23 May - Lieutenant General Sir William Howe, who had been the commander-in-chief up to this time, departed and delivered the command over to Lieutenant General Sir Henry Clinton.

6 June - A few days after having sent all the heavy baggage, as well as the tents, sick, and wives, aboard ship, the brigade of Major General von Stirn marched to the wharf not far from the upper coal magazine, from which place we were set across the Delaware in flatboats, and went on land near the ferry. We then marched six English miles and entered camp near Newton.

18 June - We marched on and entered the camp near Hatfield, where the regiment had to protect a bridge. From here we marched onward daily, entering camp near the following places:

20 June - Morristown
21 June - Mount Holly
22 June - Black Horse
23 June - Rackletown
24 June - Allingtown [Allentown ?]
25 June - to Freehold Township.
26 June - Near Freehold, where we remained. The Cornwallis Corps had a battle with the enemy at Monmouth.

28 June - We entered camp near North Swamp, where we bivouacked overnight. The following day

29 June - we made camp at Middletown.

Donop Regimental Journal

30 June - We entered camp near Navesink. We remained here until

5 July - when we were taken to the waiting transport ships in flatboats and sailed to New York, where toward

6 July - in the evening, we arrived, and the next day

7 July - debarked at the Hay Wharf on the North River and entered camp near 6-Mile Stone, on the Kingsbridge Road, not far from Marsten's Wharf. We remained here quite peacefully until

23 September - At eight o'clock in the morning the entire brigade, in accordance with orders received the previous evening, marched forward to Philipse's House, leaving the camp standing. This night the regiment bivouacked near Fort Independence, on Valentine Hill.

24 September - We arrived at Philipse's House, where we remained and bivouacked until

10 October - when we marched back to our former camp near Marsten's Wharf, arriving there at three o'clock in the afternoon.

13 October - The continuously rainy weather and the swampy ground on which the camp stood made it necessary to move the camp, so today the regiment moved its camp farther toward the East River.

9 November - In accordance with the orders received, the regiment marched to Fort Knyphausen this morning, where it is to take winter quarters in the huts built during the fall by the two regiments,, Old Lossberg and von Knyphausen.

3 June 1779 - The regiment moved out of the huts and into camp on the heights on the North River.

26 October - The regiment, which was greatly weakened by sickness from the prevailing ague throughout the local area, marched from Fort Knyphausen to John's Ferry, near Marsten's Wharf, where it was taken across the East River in flatboats to Long Island, and entered winter quarters at Bushwick.

Donop Regimental Journal

26 December - We were ordered to leave here to go to New York and were assigned quarters in the barracks there.

6 June 1780 - In accordance with orders received last night, the regiment embarked in schooners at eleven o'clock noon today at Albany Pier, and sailed to Staten Island, where it debarked and spent the night in bivouac. The baggage was left behind and each regiment took only one cannon.

7 June - The regiment was carried over to Elizabethtown Point in flatboats and formed the rear [guard] under Major General [Friedrich Wilhelm] von Lossberg. Toward evening we marched through Elizabethtown. Because the main corps, under the command of His Excellence, Lieutenant General von Knyphausen, was already returning, we marched back to the occupied place near the Point. All of this occurred during the late and dark night.

8 June - This morning the enemy attacked the English 26th Regiment and the von Donop and von Buenau Regiments were ordered to move forward to support that regiment. During this action, three men were wounded, namely: Corporal [Henrich] Harbusch, and Musketeers Theis of Colonel von Gose's Company, and [Johannes] Quans of Lieutenant Colonel HInte's Company. Because the enemy pulled back into a woods, we returned to our earlier position.

9 June - The regiment relieved the Leib Regiment and occupied the Leib Regiment's formerly occupied place.

12 June - After the army had moved forward toward Elizabethtown and taken a new posture, the regiment had to occupy the Jaeger's posts, when they moved into Elizabethtown.

17 June - During the evening the enemy fired against the regiment from 3=pound cannons, but without effect, except that a ball knocked the cane from Colonel von Gose's hand.

23 June - At daybreak the army moved forward toward Springfield, returning in the afternoon, and during the evening, it went back to Staten Island with all its baggage and artillery.

Donop Regimental Journal

During these movements the von Donop Regiment always formed the rear guard.

26 June - We were transferred from Staten Island, at Cole's Ferry, to Long Island, near Denyce's Ferry, in flatboats. We then marched from there to Brooklyn, were transferred in boats across to New York, and entered our former quarters. Orders were issued that as of today the regiment was to be in the brigade of Major General [Karl Wilhelm] von Hachenberg.

2 September - It was announced that Colonel von Gose, until this time commander of the von Donop Regiment, had been advanced to major general with the Prince Charles Regiment, and Lieutenant Colonel Hinte assumed command [of our regiment].

9 October - At five-thirty in the morning the regiment marched out of New York to Fort Knyphausen, in order to take winter quarters in the huts at that place. From now on, it is in the brigade of Major General von Gose, who has command at the fort.

17 February 1781 - It was announced that Lieutenant Colonel Heymell of the von Knyphausen Regiment had been transferred as colonel and commandant of the von Donop Regiment.

30 June - Both officers, Lieutenant von Donop and Ensign von Knoblauch, received their requested release and left the regiment.

2 October - The regiment marched out of its up-to-the-present winter cantonment in the huts to McGowan's Pass and entered the camp there, where it remained until

25 December - when it moved out of the mentioned camp and into the houses and barns lying near the East River and took winter quarters therein. Because this district was considered a part of New York, we came under the commandant at New York, Brigadier General Birch, and once again belonged to the brigade of Major General von Hachenberg.

Donop Regimental Journal

18 January 1782 - In accordance with orders received, as of today, the regiment was placed in the brigade of Major General [Ludwig] von Wurmb.

30 January - Grenadier Captain von Gall of the von Donop Regiment died of illness and was buried at New York with the customary honors.

28 April -Toward evening we suddenly received the order to be ready to embark, but no destination was mentioned.

6 May - His Excellency, Lieutenant General von Knyphausen, turned over his previously held command to His Excellence, Lieutenant General von Lossberg, and departed on

13 May - on board the frigate *Pearl*, with His Excellence, Lieutenant General Clinton, who had been relieved by General [Guy] Carleton, and set sail at once for Europe.

16 June - Nothing came of out previously given order concerning our embarkation. Instead the regiment moved out of its winter quarters at six o'clock this morning and marched to Fort Knyphausen, where the regiment was divided as follows: Colonel Hinte's Company into the barracks at Fort Knyphausen Major von Wurmb's Company in the barracks at Fort Tryon, and the three other companies, Leib, Colonel Heymell's, and Major von Kutzlevben's, camped on the heights between the two forts. Once again the regiment was under the command of Major General von Gose.

7 September - Second Lieutenant Freyenhagen, the 2nd, received his requested release. Captain Gissot received the vacant von Gall Grenadier Company, Ensign Murhard was promoted to 2nd lieutenant, and Free Corporal [Matthias] Boecking to ensign with the regiment, as of 30 May 1782.

6 November - The regiment marched to New York again and entered the winter quarters there with the non-commissioned officers and privates in the so-called "red barracks". The officers, however, were quartered with the residents of the city.

Donop Regimental Journal

8 April 1783 - At twelve o'clock noon today the King's proclamation concerning the cession of hostilities was read from the city hall by the local commandant Major Hewitson to a gathering of many thousands of people.

3 June - Lieutenant Hausmann, of the regiment, received his release as a captain.

27 September - Today the regiment received its first order to be prepared to embark for Europe.

21 November - This morning the von Donop Regiment embarked on the assigned transport ships: *Spencer*, *Montague*, and *Everly*, which lay in the North River, in the following manner:

Montague - Major General von Gose and his adjutant Lieutenant [Johann Karl Wilhelm Sittig von] Westphal, as the commander of the last brigade; Colonel Hinte, Captain von Donop, Captain von Murhard, Lieutenant von Nagel, Jr., Senior War Commissary Harnier, Lutheran Chaplain Becker, and Assistant Commissary Hatzky, and a total, including privates, wives, and children, of 194 persons.

Spencer - Colonel Heymell, Captain Geisler, Captain Venator, Lieutenant von Bardeleben, Lieutenant von Lepel, Regimental Quartermaster Zinn, Auditor Heymell, Regimental Surgeon Stieglitz, in all, with non-commissioned officers and privates, 198 persons.

Everly - Major von Wurmb, Captain Reiss, Ensign [Josef Benedikt] von Lehrbach, Ensign [Longin Karl August] von Haussen, Ensign [Karl Aemilius] Henckel, Ensign von Boecking, Chaplain Coester, and Wagonmaster [Daniel] Schulze, in all, 159 persons.

24 November - We raised anchor and sailed to Staten Island, where we remained until

26 November - During the afternoon, at two o'clock, we went under sail. By four-thirty we had passed Sandy Hook and entered the ocean.

However, already on the second day, we separated from the fleet during a strong wind and sailed onward alone and without any special occurrence until

3 January 1784 - About two o'clock in the afternoon, at a longitude of $49°49'$, a sounding found the first ground again at a depth of seventy fathoms, or 420 feet.

7 January - At about six o'clock our sailors saw the first land, namely the points in the Channel called Land's End and the Lizard.

11 January - A cutter came from Portsmouth harbor and gave us an order from the admiral that we were to enter the harbor at Portsmouth, although our first order was to make the rendezvous in The Downs, not far from Deal. Therefore we anchored this afternoon at three o'clock, near Spithead.

14 January - At nine o'clock this morning we debarked from our ship, as we were the first of our three ships which entered here, by the so-called Point, near Portsmouth, and marched through the city. Three miles distance along the London Road we entered the barracks at Hilsa.

26 January - Those of the von Donop Regiment on the ship *Montague*, with Major General von Gose, debarked, and all the rest of the men who arrived here on the 23rd of the month, arrived here in the above mentioned barracks. The reason this ship arrived later was that it had sailed directly toward Deal, as the designated rendezvous, and had then been ordered to come here. From this ship we learned that the ship *Everly*, with Major von Wurmb, had also arrived at Deal and been ordered to go to Chatham, where they were quartered in the barracks.

11 March - We received orders to be prepared to embark. The actual embarkation however was delayed until

2 April - At nine o'clock in the morning we were embarked near the Point at Portsmouth, together with some grenadiers from the von Lengercke Battalion, on board the ships *Admiral Barrington* and *Young William*, as follows:

Donop Regimental Journal

Admiral Barrington - Major General von Gose, Colonel Hinte, Captain Venator, Captain Murhard, Captain von Donop, Lieutenant von Nagel, Lieutenant von Bardeleben, Lieutenant von Westphal, [Adjutant General], Lutheran Staff Chaplain Becker, and Regimental Quartermaster Zinn.

Young William - From the von Donop Regiment - Colonel Heymell, Captain Geisler, Lieutenant von Lepel, Auditor Heymell, Regimental Surgeon Stieglitz. From the Young von Lossberg [Mirbach] Regiment - Captain [Louis Marie] von Mallet, Lieutenant [Johann Georg] Wiessenmueller, Lieutenant [Rudolph Wilhelm] Duncker, and Lieutenant [Georg Bernhard] Kersting. From the Platte Grenadier Battalion - Lieutenant [Johannes] Koerber.

8 April - This morning most of the ships of our fleet, which had been lying in the harbor until now, sailed out of the harbor, and then lay at anchor near Spithead. The agent remained lying in the harbor however, until the morning of

11 April - About eight o'clock the signal was made to set sail. The agent came out of the harbor and the entire fleet went underway. After we had sailed four days with reasonably favorable wind, we came on

15 April - at seven-thirty in the evening to anchor in the mouth of the Weser River.

16 April - About four o'clock in the morning we raised anchor and sailed close to Geestendorf near Bremerlehe, where our two ships met those of the von Loewenstein Grenadier Battalion, which had arrived from Dover Castle. After the rest of our entire fleet had arrived and assembled together, all the ships were mustered, one after the other, by the muster-master in Bremerlehe. After the muster however, we were immediately debarked from the transport ships in small boats, and went on

17 April - at three o'clock in the afternoon, up the Weser River to Bremen, where the troops on

19 April - arrived at five o'clock in the evening.

Donop Regimental Journal

22 April - All the troops embarked in the so-called "Bremer Bocke" [Bremen boats which apparently plunged up and down], from the small boats, downstream from the bridge. The regimental officers were assigned as follows in the boats.:

Numbers 19 and 20 - Colonel Heymell, Lieutenant von Lepel, Regimental Quartermaster Zinn, and Regimental Surgeon Stieglitz.

Numbers 21 and 22 - Captain Geisler, Captain Murhard, and Lieutenant von Bardeleben.

Numbers 23 and 24 - Captain Venator, Captain von Donop, and Lieutenant von Nagel, Jr..

After each boat had been assigned the appropriate number of men, they departed.

23 April - from Bremen at three o'clock in the afternoon, and most of them traveled as far as wind and weather would allow [each day].

12 May - We arrived at Hannover-Muenden, where we lay until

14 May - We landed, and, in accordance with orders received, marched to Kauffungen, Holtze, etc.

15 May - That part of the regiment that was here was mustered and on

17 May - after having had that part of the regiment which had remained behind at Chatham until 1784 rejoin us, we marched to Kassel, and into the designated barracks, where the regiment, as it is to be the garrison, is to remain.

Karl Philipp Heymell

- - - - - - -

[There is no explanation of why Auditor Heymell signed the journal, what part he may have written, nor why he is listed as the author of part of the journal.]

Index

----, Carl Hamilton Heinrich 31
    Heinrich 3
ABEL, Anna Catharina 123
    Arietha Martha Elisabeth 123
    Christoph 123
AGNEW, Brig Gen 108 Gen 106
    James 105
ALHAUS, Anna Rebecca 144
    Johann Ernst 144 Wilhelm
    Justus 144
ALMEROTH, Egidia 159
    Friedrich 159 Georg 159
AMBROSIUS, Anna Dorothea 146
AMELUNG, Surgeon 147
AMTHAUER, Reitze 142
APT, Anna Maria 153 Friedrich 153
ASHLIN, Lee 13
ASSEMANN, Elisabeth 134
AUBEL, Catharina Elisabeth 135
AUG, Susanna Magdalena 126
BARTHEL, Anna Catharina 127
    Martha Elisabeth 127 Nicolaus 127
BAUER, Johann Georg 125
    Wilhelm 118
BAURMEISTER, Carl Leopold

BAURMEISTER (cont)
    110 Maj 141-142
BAYEIX, Catherina Charlotta 148
    Cornelia 148 Mr 148
BECCKER, Chaplain 185
BECKER, Anna Catherina 145
    Anna Christina 125 Chaplain 183 Friedrich 119 Karl 119
    Peter 119 Sophie Louise 119
BERDOT, Lt 91-92 94
BERGMAN, Walteri 116-117
BERNHARD, Charlotta 132
    Michael 132
BEYER, Anna Margaretha 121
BIERHENNE, Anna Martha 148
    Conrad 147 Henrich 148
BIESENRODT, Maj 99
BIGEL, Johann Wilhelm 119
BIRCH, Brig Gen 181
BLECKWENN, Hans 117
BLESEN, Capt 130
BLOCK, Col 39 99 111 Justus
    Heinrich 15 Justus Henrich 169
BLUM, Christoph 134 Elisabeth 126 Maria Catherina 127
    Samuel 127
BODE, Capt 133 Christoph 47

BODENSTEIN, Christine
   Charlotta 120
BOECKING, Matthias 182
BOLT, Elisabeth 127
BORCK, Georg 133
BOULANGER, Anna Catherina
   154 Christina 154 Nicolaus 154
BRAND, Elisabeth Christina 151
   Regina 154
BRANDENBURG, Maria
   Catherina 153
BRAUN, Anna Catherina 128 133
BRETHAUER, Johann Henrich
   135
BURGOYNE, Gen 178
BURSCHEL, Johann 130 Sophia
   130
BUSCH, Freidrich 131 Wilhelmina
   Catharina 131
BYRD, Col 90
CALDER, Lt Col 107-108 113
CAMMARON, 13
CARLETON, Guy 182
CARTEUSER, Andreas 143
CKAUS, Dorothea 152
CLAUSING, Ludwig 131
   Wilhelmina Catharina 131
CLEVE, Ens 87
CLINTON, Henry 55 178 Lt Gen
   182
COESTER, 118 Anna Margarete
   116 Chaplain 18 44 183
   Christoph Heinrich 116
   Dorothea Wilhelmina 116 G C
   117 Georg Christian 16 122
   165 Georg Christoph 116
   Georg Christoph Bernhard 116
   Georg Christph 119 Heinrich
   Wilhelm 116 Johann Christoph

COESTER (cont)
   116 Pastor 39 92-93 105
COMPHIEL, Samuel 151
CORNWALLIS, 79 112 Charles
   55 Gen 106 Lord 104 107-108
   Lt Gen Milord 78
COSINE, Margaretha 141
COZINE, Mr 141
DALRYMPLE, William 54
DEBARDELEBEN, John F 2
DECKER, Justus 134
DELALIME, Charlotta 132
DELANCEY, Oliver 67
DESCOURDES, Catherina
   Charlotta 148 Cornelia 148
   Louis 149
DICKHAUT, Anna Gerdruth 129
   157 Henrich Reihard 157
   Johannes 153 Leonora Luisa
   129 Werner 129 157
DIEKMANN, 101
DIETRICH, Elisabeth 146 Jacob
   142 Maria Margaretha 142
   Martha Catharina 142
DIETZEL, Lt 149 Mrs 149
DITMAR, Anna Elisabeth 159
   Catherina Elisabeth 139
   Johann Wilhelm 139
DOENSTAEDT, 148 Anna
   Martha 148
DONOP, Capt 87
DUNCKER, Rudolph Wilhelm 185
DUPUY, Maj 147
EBERHARD, Cannoneer 140
   David 151 Dorothea Elisabeth
   140 151 Johann Valentin 151
EBERT, Dr 119 Johannes 151
   Maria Elisabeth 151
EGO, Mr 31

EICHENAUER, Anton 145
EICHLER, 157 Elisabeth 157
EICHLERS, Elisabeth 139 Jost 139
EISMANN, Margaretha 125
EITEL, Hans Heinrich 15 Hans Henrich 141 Lt Col 155
EMLOTH, Anna Elisabeth 156 Johannes 156
ENGELHARD, Christian 137 Eva Barbara 137-138 Johann Valentin 137
ENGLAND, King Of 34 102
ERB, Dorothea Elisabeth 124
EREMATEICH, Eusebrius 156 Johanna Rosina Justina 156
ERNST, Justus Heinrich 47
ERSKINE, Gen 96 William 55
ESKUCHE, Dr 111 Karl 110
ESKUCKE, Anna Catherina Elisabeth 119 Balthasar Ludwig 119 Catherina Florentine 119 Johann Christoph 119
EWALD, Capt 153-154 Johann 109 126
FALKENER, Mrs 138
FAUCHER, Catherina Florentine 119
FAUCITT, Col 167-168 William 14
FEHR, Johann Georg 134
FERDINAND, Arthur Franz 2
FLASCHAAR, Anna Gerdruth 147 Wihelm 147
FOCK, Annette Luzie Margaretha 149 Georg Henrich 149 Maria Catherina 149
FREY, Anna Margaretha 135 151 Conrad 135 Elisabeth Christina

FREY (cont)
151 Georg Adolf 135 Georg Adolph 151 156 Johann Georg 156 Margaretha 156
FREYENHAGEN, 19 Ens 17 80 173 Karl August Sr 16 164 Lt 105 Lt 2nd 182 Wilhelm Johann Ernst Jr 16 164
FREYTAG, Georg 143 Gerdruth 143 Johann Caspar 143
FRIDERICK, Maria Catherina 137
FRIEDRICH II, Prince Of Hesse-Cassel 117
FRISE, David 125
FUCHS, Maria Sebina 129 Pastor 129
FUEHRER, Karl Friedrich 148
FUELLGRAFF, Anna Gerdruth 152 Gerhard 152 Johannes 152
GALL, Capt 89
GASSERT, Eva Catherina 139 Joseph 139 Kilian 139
GEBHARD, Anna Catherina 150
GEISE, Anton 141
GEISLER, Capt 183 185-186 Friedrich Wilhelm 16 Friedrick Wilhelm 164
GEMELING, 132
GEORGE II, King Of England 117
GEORKE, Casimir Theodor 141 Elisabeth 141
GERMER, Johann Anton 47
GIEBEL, A 116-117
GIESE, Conrad 132
GILSA, 89
GISSOT, Capt 18 28 80 173 182 Johann Matthias 16 165
GLEIM, Anna Elisabeth 159 Elisabeth 159 Johannes 159

GOEBEL, Capt 140
GOERKE, Casimir Theodor 132
   Elisabeth 132 Henriette 141
GOTTLOB, Johannes Franziscus
   152
GRAGES, Dorothea Elisabeth 144
   Johann Henrich 144 Sophia
   Wilhelmina 144
GRANT, Gen 73 James 59 70
GRAY, Maj 108
GREY, Charles 105 Gen 108 Maj
   Gen 106
GRIMM, 87 91 105 David 86
   Maria Elisabeth 86 Mr 92
   Peggy 86
GRIMMEL, Anna Catherina
   Elisabeth 119 Anna Juiana 120
   Johann Conrad 119 Martin 119
GROMANN, Dorothea Elisabeth
   125 Johannes 125
GROSS, Conrad 150 Johanna
   Margaretha 150
GUEMBELL, Anna Elisabeth 126
   128 157 Philipp 126 128 157
HAAK, Corp 144 Sophia
   Wilhelmina 144
HABBLER, Johann Jost 133
HAEMER, Hamilton Carl Heinrich
   122 Johannes 122 129 Maria
   Elisabeth 122 129
HAMILTON, Capt 18 88 William
   122
HANCK, Maria Wilhelmina 157
   Wilhelmina 140
HANCKEN, Maria Wilhelmina
   148
HARBUSCH, Henrich 180
HARCOURT, William 83
HARNIER, Senior War

HARNIER (cont)
   Commisary 183
HARS, Anna Elisabeth 129 156
HARTMANN, Anna Elisabeth 126
   Christina 126 Jacob 126
HARTWIG, Anna Catherina 141
   Eva Catherina Sophia 141
   Johann Friedrich 141
HASE, Anna Elisabeth 126
   Conrad 126 Johann Georg 126
HASELBACH, Elisabeth 137
HASSENPFLUG, Anna Catherina
   144 Catharina Elisabeth 123
   Conrad 144 Johann 123
HATZKY, Asst Commisary 183
HAUSKNECHT, Chaplain 123
   Christine Maria Anna 120
   Johann Georg 111 120 Johann
   Wilhelm 120
HAUSMANN, Emanual Rosinus
   16 Emanuel Rosinus 164 Lt 17
   72 80 173 183
HAYNLEIN, Anna Catherina 137
   Georg 137 Maria Catherina
   137
HEIDMUELLER, Johann Justus
   144
HEINBECK, Anna Catherina 155
   Daniel 155 Johannes Stephen
   155
HEINRICH, Johann 2
HELLER, Capt 36 Chaplain 126
HELMERICH, Georg Wilhelm 144
HELMRICH, Gerdruth 127
HELWIG, A 116-117
HENCE, David 125 Johann
   Reinhard 125 Margaretha 125
HENCKEL, Karl Aemilius 183
HENCKLEIN, Maria Catherina

HENCKLEIN (cont)
145
HERD, Anna Elisabeth 123
HERDMANN, Johann Valentin
138
HERINGEN, Col 67
HERMANN, Anna Catherina 142
Corp 142
HESSEMUELLER, Capt 145
HESSLER, Anna Catherina 128
Johannes 128 133 Mnaria
Catharina 133
HEWITSON, Maj 183
HEYMELL, Auditor 18 130 173
183 185 Bartholomai Ernst 16
165 Col 139 141 156-157 173
183 185-186 Karl Philipp 3 9
122 186 Lt Col 10-11 13-14 16
18 25 31 74 102-103 128-129
167 181
HILDEBRAND, Sophie Louise
119
HINTE, Col 134 147 182-183 185
Erasmus Ernst 16 165 Lt Col
180-181 Maj 17 36 44 74 81
102 128 167 173
HIRSCH, Anna Margaretha 139
Catherina Elisabeth 139
Conrad 139
HOFFER, Anton 145 Catherina
Elisabeth 145 Johann Henrich
145
HOHENSTEIN, Capt 133 145
HOLZAPFEL, Johann 133
HOLZMUELLER, Christoph 152
Dorothea 152 Johannes
Franziscus 152
HOTHAM, William 26 168
HOWE, Gen 55 93 114 Gen Lord

HOWE (cont)
75 104 Lord 106 Lt Gen 67 71
73 105 Lt Gen Lord 74 84
Richard 175 William 173 178
HUENE, Johann Henrich Gottfried
126
HUETHER, Friedrich 151
HUMBURG, Anna Maria 153
Christoph 126 Elisabeth 126
Henrich Wilhelm 126 Valentin
151
HUND, Anna Gerdruth 147
Conrad 147 Martha Catherina
147
HUNDESHAGEN, Anna
Catherina 121
HUNOLD, Johannes 147 Philipp
147
IDE, Anna Elisabeth 128 Johannes
128
IFFERT, Catherina Elisabeth 125
Johann Henrich 125 144 Jost
Henrich 145 Maria Catherina
145 Valentin 145
INDIAN, Jarock 130
JACOB, Anna Martha 128
JACOBI, Friderica Ludwig 143
JOHANN, Adam Kurz 127
JOHN, Mr 172
JOHNS, 70
JONES, 70
KAHLSTUETZER, Eva Barbara
137-138
KASSEL, 19
KATZMANN, 155 Eva 140 155
Johann Caspar 140 143
Johannes 140
KAUFHOLD, Anna Catherina 155
KAYSER, Lt 173

KEHL, Henrich 129 Maria Sebina 129
KERSTING, Georg Bernhard 185 Johann Christian 146
KEYSER, Lt 17 80
KILIAN, Conrad 133
KIP, Eva 155 Gottfried 155
KLEE, Kilian 139
KLEINSCHMIDT, Gerdruth 143 Karl August 36 Lt 47
KLINGENDEN, Friedrich 154
KNOBLAUCH, Ens 168
KOCH, Adam 125 Berthold 127 Grenadier 133 Maria Dorothea 125 Wilhelm Philipp 125
KOEHLER, Johann Heinrich 120
KOERBEL, 153 Eva Elisabeth 153
KOERBER, Johannes 185
KRAFFT, Christine Maria Anna 120 Justus Christoph 120
KRAMER, Johann Henrich 133
KRAUSE, Christian 126 H 116-117
KRUECK, Anna Catherina 124 Henrich 158 Johann 124 Johannes 158
KRUESCHEL, Maria Amalia 153 Otto Friedrich 153
KRUG, Georg 99
KUEMMEL, Johann Kaspar 114
KUEMMELL, 118 Adam Friedrich 120 Chaplain 159 Christina Margaretha 120 Christine Charlotta 120 Henrich 120
KUMELL, Lt 90
KUNIGUNDE, Anna 141
KURZ, Anna Catharina 123 Anna Catherina 127 129 137 140 154

KURZ (cont) Joachim 123 127 129 137 140 154 Johann Adam 123 Johann Henrich 154
KUTZLEBEN, Maj 139
LALIME, John Baptiste 132
LANDAU, Christina 126
LEE, Charles 83
LEISNER, Maria Catherina 149
LENTZ, Elisabeth 143 Johannes 143
LEPEL, Lt 17
LEPNER, Mr 86-87 89 110
LESLIE, Alexander 55 Brig Gen 108 Gen 106
LETZERICH, Johann 130 Martha 130
LEYTMEIER, Rosina Charlotta 131
LINNINGER, Eva Catherina 139
LOCKBERGER, Anna Catherina 154 Christian 154 Johannes 154
LOEHLER, Abraham 130 Elisabeth 130
LOHR, Maria Elisabeth 122 129
LOREY, Johann Friedrich 145
LOSCH, Anna Maria 153
LUDOLPH, Carl 131 Rosina Charlotta 131
LUDWIG, Christopher 2 Gertrutha Sophia 128 Reinhard 128
LUMPE, Johannes 124
MAERTEN, Andreas 142 Anna Gerdruth 142 Henrich 142
MANGOLD, Anna Catherina 150 Hans Christoph 150 Johanna Margaretha 149
MARKHAM, Lt Col 106

MARTIN, Anna Catharina 123
MATHEW, Edward 106 Gen 108
MAWHOOD, Charles 106
MAY, Anna Catherina 144
   Christina 154 Johann Galenus
   144 Wilhelmina Leonora 144
MAYER, Eva 140
MEIEN, 130 Sophia 130
MELSHEIMER, Chaplain 118
MENTLER, Jacob 155
MENTZLER, Anna Catherina 155
MERTEN, Anna Gerdruth 132
   Henrich 131
METZER, Maria Magdalena 125
   Sgt 125
MOHR, Barbara Elisabeth 147
   Philippus 147
MORITZ, Dorothea Elisabeth 144
MOTZ, 47
MUEHLHAUSEN, Johann
   Christoph 73
MUENSTER, Anna Maria 147
MUHLENBERG, Peter 95
MURHARD, Capt 185-186 Ens
   173 182 Lt 17 81 173 Philipp
   Heinrich 16
MURRAY, 137
NAGEL, Lt Jr 103 Lt Sr 19 51
NAUMANN, Bernhard 138
NEUMANN, Capt 145
NUMME, Conrad 136
OBERSTEIG, Maria Magdalena
   126
OHM, Wilhelmina Catharina 131
OPFER, Conrad 157
OSTHEIM, Johannes 148
OTTO, Angelica Dorothea 124
   Anna Catherina 124 Johann
   Heinrich 124

PARKER, Agent 168
PATTERSON, Sarah 138 Stephen
   138
PAUER, Isabella 160 Mary 160
   Merry 160 Thomas 160
PAULY, Catherina Elisabeth 137
   Elisabeth 137 Johann Dietrich
   137
PEACOCK, Capt 17 Robert 122
PEFFER, Wilhelmina 121
PELOTROW, Maria Elisabeth 151
PERCY, Hugh 55 Lt Gen 70
PFAFF, Johann Adam 154 156
PFLUEGER, Anna Elisabeth 128
   157 Elisabeth 159 Johann 135
   Mrs 139
PHEIL, Conrad 142 Martha
   Catherina 142
PICKHARD, Anna Gerdruth 129
   157
PLAAUMENS, Elisabeth 160
POST, Anna 141 Anton 140 Georg
   140
PRUESCHENCK, Maj 130
QUANS, Johannes 180
RALL, Col 82 172 Johann Gottlieb
   50
REDLY, Capt 17
REICHHARD, Johann Henrich
   141
REIMANN, Christina Margaretha
   120 Georg Philipp 120
REISS, Capt 183 Johann Philipp
   16 164 Lt 173
REITZE, Anna Catherina 142
REYERS, Anna Catharina 142
   Anna Maria 142 Georg
   Henrich 142
RHEIDER, 149 Andreas 149

RHEIDER (cont)
   Barbara 149
RIEHL, Anna Martha 129 Conrad 129
RIEL, Anna Catherina 128 Maria Catharina 133
RIMMEL, Anna Martha 129
RINCKE, Margaretha Barbara 152
RITBERGER, Anna Catherina 148
ROBERTSON, James 65
ROEHRSCHEIT, Anna Dorothea 146 Corp 146 Elisabeth 146
ROEM, Anna Catherina 148 Henrich Reinhard 148 157 Martha 148
ROEMER, Heinrich Philipp 123 Martha Elisabeth 123 127 Reinhardi 127
ROESE, Henrich 134
ROOSEVEL, Elisabeth 132
ROOSEVELT, Elisabeth 132
ROSENTHAL, Anna Margaretha 151 Margaretha 156
ROTH, Catherina Elisabeth 147 Grenadier 147
RUMMEL, Christian Conrad 152 Margaretha Barbara 152 Philipp Adam 152
RUPPORT, Johann Adam 154 Michael 154 Regina 154
SACKERT, Carolina 130 Conrad 130
SADLER, Anna Maria 142
SANDMOELLER, Catherina Elisabeth 137 Friedrich 137
SCHAEFER, Anna Elisabeth 159 Henrich 159
SCHAEFFER, Martha Elisabeth 159

SCHANZ, Anna Martha 129
SCHEELE, Bertold 127 Christian 127 Elisabeth 127
SCHEFFER, Anna Elisabeth 123 129 156 Catharina Elisabeth 123 Col 144 Conrad 148 Dorothea Elisabeth 140 Elisabeth 122 157 Johann Heinrich 122 Johannes 123 129 148 156 Maria Wilhelmina 148 157 Wilhelm 140 148 157 Wilhelmina 140
SCHEFFLER, Robert 122
SCHEUER, Anna Martha 129
SCHEURL, Anna Rosina 146
SCHICK, Anna Gerdruth 132 152
SCHLEESTEIN, Capt 140 148 151 155 157
SCHMECK, Adam 124 128 141 153 Anna Catherina 141 Anna Martha 124 128 141-142 153 Johann Adam 127 Johannes 124 153
SCHMID, Anna Maria 153 Caspar 153 Eva Elisabeth 152 War Cashier 105
SCHMIDT, Catherina Elisabeth 124 Dorothea Elisabeth 124 Hautboist Johann Ludwig 153 Johann Henrich 154 Johannes 124 Maria Amalia 153 Maria Catherina 153 Martin 14
SCHNEIDER, Catherina 128 Col 149
SCHOTTEN, Lt 107
SCHRECKER, Heinrich 121 Johann Konrad Heinrich 121
SCHREIBER, Anna Catherina 154 Johann Wilhelm 15

SCHROEDER, Anna Catherina
    128 133 140 148 158 Bernhard
    134 Georg 128 133 140 158
    Johannes 134 Wilhelm 128 148
SCHUCHARD, Adam 128 Anna
    Martha 128
SCHUCK, Anna Catherina 145
    Anna Christina 125 Johann
    Paulus 125 Maria Magdalena
    125 Sgt 145
SCHUENTZ, Anna Maria 147
SCHUETZ, Catherina Elisabeth
    147 Johannes 147 152
SCHULTHEISS, Eva Catherina
    Sophia 141
SCHULTZ, Daniel 17 100
    Wagonmaster 17
SCHULZE, Daniel 183
SCHUNACHER, Gerdruth 155
SCHWARZ, Johann Georg 124
SCHWARZBACH, Anna
    Catharina 127
SCHWEIN, Johannes 75
SEHNER, Anna Maria 145
SEHRS, Anna Rebecca 144
SEIDLING, Corp 155-156 Rosina
    155-156
SELZAM, Daniel 155
SPOHR, Conrad 134
STANGE, Anna Catharina 158
    Catherina Elisabeth 125
    Catherina Friderica 143
    Catherina Friederica 158
    Christoph 143 158 Dorothea
    Elisabeth 125 Peter 125
STARK, Angelica Dorothea 124
STEDING, Adam Chrisstoph 36
STERN, Georg Christian 121
    Wilhelmina Juliana 121

STEUBER, Catherina Elisabeth
    145
STIEGELITZ, Johann Jacob 16
    Reg Surgeon 17
STIEGLITZ, Johann Jacob 127
    Johann Jakob 165 Surgeon 183
    185-186
STIRLING, Lt Col 108 113
    Thomas 107
STIRN, Gen 64 70 78 101-102 104
    108 Johann Daniel 14 171 Maj
    Gen 105 173
STOEBEL, Georg 101
SUSTMAN, Johannes 129
SUSTMANN, Adam 123 Johann
    Adam 133 Maria Elisabeth 129
    133
THIEL, Anna Catherina 145 Anna
    Maria 145 Georg 145
THOMAS, Christoph 134
THOMPSON, Friedrich Henrich
    145
THOMSON, Mr 145 Sally 145
TIEZEN, Polly 135
TILLEMANN, 11
TIPPEL, Dorothea Elisabeth 151
TOERFELS, Corp 130 Leonora
    Luisa 130
TRAUTWEIN, Annette Luzie
    Margaretha 149 Johannes 149
TRELAWNEY, Lt Col 106 108
TRINKETRUG, Barbara Elisabeth
    147 Gerhard 147
TRISCHMANN, Catherina 128
    Paul 128
TRUEMPER, Anna Elisabeth 133
TRUMPF, Abel 124 Angelica
    Dorothea 124 Anna Christina
    124 Johann Georg 124

TUCK, Mr 138
TWISLETON, Lt Col 108 112-113
TYRON, William 96
ULRICH, Johannes 154 Rosina
  155-156
UNGEWITTER, Reinhard
  Friedrich 17
VANMUELLER, Martha Elisabeth
  148
VAUGHAN, Gen 106 108 John
  105
VENATOR, Capt 17 19 23 34 51
  59 88 103 168 173 183 185-
  186 Justus Friedrich 16 145
  165
VIEMANN, Anna Catharina 123
  Anna Catherina 127 129 137
  140 154
VILLGRAFF, Anna Gerdruth 132
  Erhard 132
VILMANN, Pastor 127
VIRNAU, Anna Margaretha 121
  Johannes 121 Wilhelm
  Reinhard 121 Wilhelmina 121
VOGELER, Johannes 140
VOGELEY, Martha Catharina 155
VOGT, Bernhard 138 Christiana
  Sophia 138 Jacob 138
VOLHARS, Anna Martha 128
VONALTEN-BAKUM, Capt 144
VONANDERSON, Ernst Wilhelm
  17 Lt 90
VONBARDELEBEN, Arthur
  Franz Ferdinand 2 Carolina 89
  Franz Ferdinand 3 Johann
  Heinrich 2-4 16 116 122
  Johann Henrich 165 Lt 18 183
  185-186
VONBIRSCHHAUSEN, Karl

VONBIRSCHHAUSEN (cont)
  Ernst 15
VONBISCHHAUSEN, Col 146
VONBOECKING, Ens 183
VONBORCK, Heinrich 15
VONBOSE, Karl 15
VONCOCHENHAUSEN, Johann
  Friedrich 110
VONDERLIPPE, Count 47 Simon
  Ludwig Wilhelm 36
VONDONOP, Capt 16-17 74 154
  173 183 185-186 Christoph
  Dietrich 9 165 Col 60 82 130
  170 Fraeulein 9 Karl Emil
  Ulrich 14-15 Lt 9 16-17 181
  Wilhelm Heinrich August 100
  Wilhelm Henrich 164 Wilhelm
  Karl 7 165
VONEBENAUER, Lt 145
VONESCHWEGE, Capt 105 Lt 90
VONEWALD, Capt 125
VONGALL, Capt 17 80 126 135
  146 182 Philipp Wilhelm 16
  164 Wilhelm Philipp 125
VONGILSA, 2 Carolina 89
  Charlotha 89 Fraeulein 9 Lt 89
VONGOSE, Col 17 93 101 103
  123 127-129 148 173 180-181
  Col Com 16 David Ephraim 15
  165 Maj Gen 136 139 143 151
  181-185 Maj Gen Baron 156
VONHACHENBERG, Col 90 Karl
  Wilhelm 15 114 181
VONHANSTEIN, Ludwig August
  131
VONHAUSSEN, Longin Karl
  August 183
VONHEISTER, Gen 103 108
  Leopold 14 124 174 Lt Gen 14

VONHEISTER (cont)
 20 34 55 57 63 70 87 101 104-
 105 112
VONHERINGEN, Heinrich Anton
 54
VONHERINGER, Henrich Anton
 15
VONHEYMELL, Col 132 Karl
 Philipp 165
VONHINTE, Maj 122
VONHUYN, Col 77
VONKNOBLAUCH, Ens 18 23 81
 173 181 Karl 16 165
VONKNYPHAUSEN, Gen 103 Lt
 Gen 71 73-76 156 180 182
VONKUTZLEBEN, Capt 23 123
 128-129 Christian Moritz 16
 Maj 127 131 137 140 154 157
 167
VONKUTZLEVBEN, Maj 182
VONLEHRBACH, Josef Benedikt
 183
VONLENGERCKE, Col 139 157
VONLEPEL, Lt 103 172-173 183
 185-186 Wilhelm 16
VONLINSING, Otto Christian
 Wilhelm 15
VONLOEWENSTEIN, Wilhelm
 131
VONLOOS, Col 130 Johann
 August 104
VONLOSSBERG, Col 54 71 77
 Ens 17 19 Friedrich Wilhelm
 14-15 132 180 Jeremias 16 Lt
 103 173 Lt Gen 182
VONMALLET, Capt 146-147 152
 159 Louis Marie 185
VONMINNIGERODE, Col 124
 Friedrich Ludwig 15 105

VONMIRBACH, Werner 14 50
VONMUENCHHAUSEN, Col 127
VONMURHARD, Capt 183
VONNAGEL, 173 Heinrich
 Ludwig Sr 16 Henrich Ludwig
 Jr 165 Karl Friedrich 16 Karl
 Friedrich Sr 165 Lt 185 Lt Jr
 17 23 81 88 90 168 183 186 Lt
 Sr 17 23 34 81 168 172
VONPRUENSCHENCK, Lt Col
 155
VONRALL, Johann Gottlieb 50
VONRAU, Karl 73
VONROEDER, Capt 152
VONSCHIECK, Ernst Rudolph 59
 Lt Col 85-86
VONSTADELL, Ens 17 Franz
 Karl 16
VONSTAEDEL, Ens 169 Franz
 Karl 165
VONSTAEDELL, 16
VONSTEIN, Capt 134
VONSTEINZUALTENSTEIN,
 Johann Andreas Karl 86 Maria
 Elisabeth 86
VONSTIRN, Gen 175 177 Maj
 Gen 178
VONSTUCKROD, 89
VONTROTT, Eitel Wilhelm 16
 165 Ens 18 80-81 92 173
VONURFF, Christian 86
VONWALDENFELS, Capt 152
 Christoph Friedrich 145
VONWANGENHEIM, Friedrich
 Adam Julius 126
VONWEITERSHAUSEN, Capt 16
 79-80 Friedrich Karl 10 124
 164
VONWESTPHAL, Johann Karl

VONWESTPHAL (cont)
    Wilhelm Sittig 183 Lt 185
VONWILMOWSKY, Capt 158
VONWREDEN, Karl August 109
VONWURMB, Col 103 107
    Friedrich Wilhelm 36 Lt Col
    153 156 Ludwig 182 Maj 140
    148 153 155 158 183-184
VONZUMPITZ, Anna Rosina 146
    Dillman Jacob 146 Wilhelm
    Philipp 146
WACH, Capt 130 146
WACHER, Corp 130 Martha 130
WACKER, Martha 130
WAGNER, Johann Friedrich
    Zacharias 88 Johann Georg 156
WAHL, Anna Martha 129
    Johannes 129
WALDECK, Chaplain 118
WALDENBERGER, Peter Michael
    34
WALLES, Capt 17
WALTENBERG, Capt 127
WASHINGTON, 82 Gen 104
WEBER, Anna Elisabeth 128
    Georg 133 Henrich Sr 134
WEETE, Anna Margarete 116
    Mathias 116
WEHRMENN, Georg 39
WEIDEMANN, Anna Catherina
    121 Johann Christoph 121
WEIDERMANN, Pastor 127
WEISE, Anton 146 Elisabeth 146
    Johann Christian Friedrich 146
WEISING, Gerdruth 127 Jost
    Henrich 127 Maria Catharina
    127
WEITERSHAUSEN, Capt 129
WELL, Christian 134 Elisabeth

WELL (cont)
    130
WENDEROTH, Anna Catherina
    135
WENIG, Philipp Adam 152
WERNER, Anna Catherina 141
    Johann 141
WERNERT, Anna Martha 129
    Henrich 129
WETZLER, Carolina 130
WICKS, Anna Maria 153
    Dorothea Christina 153 Johann
    Christopher 153
WIEDERHOLD, Catharina
    Elisabeth 123 Maria Elisabeth
    123 129 133
WIEGANDT, Anna Martha 148
WIELTECK, Friederica Heinerica
    125 Johannn Georg 125 Joseph
    Karl 125
WIESLER, Johannes 121
    Wilhelmina Juliana 121
WIESSENMUELLER, Johann
    Georg 185
WINCKELMANN, Ludwig 69
WIRTH, Gerdruth 126 Johann
    Friedrich 126 Peter Paul 126
WIRTHS, Gerdruth 155 Peter Paul
    155 Rosina 155
WOLFF, Henrich 128
WORINGER, August 118
WREDE, Capt 145
ZEHR, Burghard 135
ZELAZIN, Gertrutha Sophia 128
ZERTS, Elisabeth 139 Johannes
    139 Mrs 139
ZINN, Johann Georg 16 162 164-
    165 Reg Quartermaster 17 183
    185-186

THE AUTHOR

Bruce E. Burgoyne was born 25 October 1924 in Benton Harbor, Michigan, and is married with three grown sons. His wife Marie, a Doctor of Education from the University of Southern California, is a helpful research companion and source of encouragement. Mr. Burgoyne's education includes a Master of Arts in Social Science (History, Economics, and Government) from Trinity University in San Antonio, Texas, plus course work at half a dozen other colleges and universities in America and overseas. He has also completed numerous military courses in such subjects as German language, Counterintelligence, and Public Information.

His employment, in addition to recently teaching a seminar course on the Hessians at Delaware State University, has included twenty years of military service in the Navy, Army, and Air Force, and six years as a civilian intelligence officer with the Army. During his military and civilian service he lived six years in Germany during which time he attended German language school in Oberammergau and two months of in-depth study, living in German households and undergoing Berlitz-type training. His daily duties required interviewing and interrogating in German, which further developed his knowledge of the language.

His forty years of research on the role of the Hessians in the American Revolutionary War have taken him and his wife to archives in England and Holland, as well as those in Germany and the United States, and resulted in the translation of more than 35 major Hessian documents.

Other Heritage Books by Bruce E. Burgoyne:

*A Hessian Officer's Diary of the American Revolution
Translated from an Anonymous Ansbach-Bayreuth Diary and the Prechtel Diary*

Canada During the American Revolutionary War: Lieutenant Friedrich Julius von Papet's Journal of the Sea Voyage to North America and the Campaign Conducted There

CD: A Hessian Diary of the American Revolution

CD: A Hessian Officer's Diary of The American Revolution

CD: A Hessian Report on the People, the Land, the War of Eighteenth Century America, as Noted in the Diary of Chaplain Philipp Waldeck, 1776-1780

CD: Ansbach-Bayreuth Diaries from the Revolutionary War

CD: Canada During the America Revolutionary War

CD: Diaries of Two Ansbach Jaegers

CD: The Hessian Collection, Volume 1: Revolutionary War Era

CD: They Also Served. Women with the Hessian Auxiliaries

CD: Waldeck Soldiers of the American Revolutionary War

Defeat, Disaster, and Dedication

Diaries of Two Ansbach Jaegers

Eighteenth Century America (A Hessian Report on the People, the Land, the War) as Noted in the Diary of Chaplain Philipp Waldeck (1776-1780)

Enemy Views: The American Revolutionary War as Recorded by the Hessian Participants

English Army and Navy Lists Compiled During the American Revolutionary War by Ansbach-Bayreuth Lieutenant Johann Ernst Prechtel

Georg Pausch's Journal and Reports of the Campaign in America, as Translated from the German Manuscript in the Lidgerwood Collection in the Morristown Historical Park Archives, Morristown, New Jersey

Hesse-Hanau Order Books, a Diary and Roster: A Collection of Items Concerning the Hesse-Hanau Contingent of "Hessians" Fighting Against the American Colonists in the Revolutionary War

Hessian Chaplains: Their Diaries and Duties

Hessian Letters and Journals and a Memoir

Journal of a Hessian Grenadier Battalion

Journal of the Hesse-Cassel Jaeger Corps

Journal of the Prince Charles Regiment
Translated by Bruce E. Burgoyne; Edited by Dr. Marie E. Burgoyne

Most Illustrious Hereditary Prince: Letters to Their Prince from Members of Hesse-Hanau Military Contingent in the Service of England During the American Revolution

Notes from a British Museum

Order Book of the Hesse-Cassel von Mirbach Regiment

Revolutionary War Letters Written by Hessian Officers: Generals Wilhelm von Knyphausen, Carl Wilhelm Von Hachenberg, Friedrich Wilhelm von Lossberg, Johann Friedrich Cochenhausen, Friedrich Von Riedesel and Major Carl Leopold von Baurmeister
Bruce E. Burgoyne and Dr. Marie E. Burgoyne

The Diary of Lieutenant von Bardeleben and Other von Donop Regiment

The Hesse-Cassel Mirbach Regiment in the American Revolution

The Third English-Waldeck Regiment in the American Revolutionary War

The Trenton Commanders: Johann Gottlieb Rall and George Washington, as Noted in Hessian Diaries

Waldeck Soldiers of the American Revolutionary War

www.ingramcontent.com/pod-product-compliance
Lightning Source LLC
Chambersburg PA
CBHW070739160426
43192CB00009B/1505